'**home truth**: a woundin̲g̲ ̲.̲.̲.̲ ̲w̲e̲a̲k̲n̲e̲s̲s'

– Shorter Oxford Dictionary

Home Truths was first performed at the Birmingham
Repertory Theatre on 13 February 1998. It
was directed by Tony Clark, designed by Fran
Thompson, with lighting by Tim Mitchell. The cast
was as follows:

ADRIAN LUDLOW	Brian Protheroe
ELEANOR LUDLOW	Margot Leicester
SAMUEL SHARP	Cliff Howells
FANNY TARRANT	Rachel Pickup

I am grateful to several people who read and
commented on the play at various stages of its
composition – Leah Schmidt, Mike Shaw, David
Edgar, Alison Lurie, Mike Ockrent, and especially
Tony Clark – and to my talented and committed
cast for their valuable contributions in rehearsals.

DL

INTRODUCTION

Like most writers, I usually get my ideas for fiction from my own experience. Some segment or episode of my life – being a visiting professor in America at the height of the Student Revolution, say (*Changing Places*), or joining the international conference circuit (*Small World*) – seems to contain thematic possibilities of general interest which I try to explore through a fictional story. Usually this process entails moving a considerable number of characters through time and space in a complex and expansive plot, requiring the scope and flexibility of the novel form.

When writing for the stage (something I have attempted only twice to date) I start with a situation which I have experienced, but which is selected primarily because it lends itself to being enacted (rather than narrated) by a small number of characters, in a few segments of 'real time', and in the same place. I am aware that this is a very conservative concept of the theatrical, but as a relative beginner in this form I find it useful to work within the constraints of the well-made play. In my first, *The Writing Game*, the situation with which I started was a short residential creative writing course, which one of the characters compares to 'a pressure cooker'. In my new play, *Home Truths*, which also focuses on professional writers, it is the journalistic interview. Two interviews are featured in the play: one provokes another, with unpredictable consequences for all concerned.

The interview is an inherently dramatic, necessarily dialogic encounter between two people, though it may involve others. It can have many subtexts, and be driven by a variety of motives. It can be a transaction, a seduction, a game, a struggle, a collusion, a confession – or perhaps all these things in turn.

The 'celebrity interview' was a development of late-nineteenth-century journalism – first in America, and then in Britain. It has been a staple ingredient of newspapers and magazines ever since, being a relatively simple and cheap way of filling column inches, and an effective means of imparting 'human interest' to the reporting of political, social and cultural events and trends. But although it is not a new phenomenon, the interview has certainly

[1] First published in the *Sunday Telegraph*, 15 February 1998, under the title 'I'm interviewed, therefore I am'.

become more ubiquitous and influential in recent times, for two obvious reasons. The first is the exponential increase in the media of communication brought about by modern technology – newspapers with all their special 'sections' and 'supplements', magazines aimed at every possible niche in the market, and the innumerable channels, programmes and websites accessible by television, radio and the Internet. The second reason is the importance of publicity in the modern world, and the way in which the presentation of personality through the media crucially determines success and failure in political, social and cultural life. What happens when the President of the United States is threatened with a politically damaging scandal? The First Lady goes on breakfast television and defends him . . . in an interview.

Politicians and stars of show business have long been accustomed to giving interviews, but writers – or at least literary writers – have attracted this kind of media attention on a large scale comparatively recently. I don't myself recall giving an interview to a newspaper journalist before 1980, when my sixth novel was published. The great masters of modern literature, like James Joyce, D. H. Lawrence, Joseph Conrad or Virginia Woolf, were seldom, if ever, interviewed in the press. When the little magazine *Paris Review* began to publish question-and-answer interviews with distinguished writers in the 1950s, it was considered a novelty. Nowadays, however, every publisher of literary fiction employs 'publicists' whose job it is to secure as many media interviews as possible for their authors when a new book is coming out, and the latter may be contractually obliged to co-operate. Playwrights, screenplay writers, poets – artists of all kinds – are apt to be involved in the same process. The interview has become a key element in the circulation and reception of what used to be called 'high culture'.

Some writers may enjoy this kind of attention, at least until the novelty wears off; but most regard it as a professional chore, and some may feel threatened by it. Saul Bellow once described interviews as like thumbprints on his windpipe. Very few authors, however, refuse to give any interviews at all. Very few, perhaps, can afford to.

Every interview is a kind of contest between the interviewee, who wants to present a certain version of himself or herself to the world, and the interviewer, who wants to discover something new and revealing about the subject. But this tension is especially acute where the activity of writing is involved. As I said above, fiction usually arises out of one's inner or outer life, but writers use various masks, rhetorical devices and narrative transpositions to conceal this process, so that the finished work may stand on its own two feet, with its own imaginative life. The interview threatens to undo this laborious work. It seeks to disprove T. S. Eliot's famous assertion that verbal art is 'not the expression of personality, but an escape from personality'. And it has done so, lately, by borrowing many of the techniques of literary fiction.

Interviews are seldom simple question-and-answer affairs these days. Instead the interviewer will use all kinds of novelistic devices to describe the subject, his physiognomy, habitat, clothing, body-language, etc., etc. The interviewer herself (interestingly, it is a journalistic field dominated by women) often features as a character in the Story of the Interview, revealing her thoughts before, during and after the encounter, and sometimes reflecting on the conventions of the whole business in a self-conscious, post-modernist way. And in the last decade some interviewers have made a name for themselves by being devastatingly critical of their subjects, employing a mocking and satirical style.

In this latter respect the interview merely reflects a general trend in the quality press over the last decade or so: a kind of gossipy spitefulness, a gloating pleasure in the imputed failings or failures of those who are newsworthy in the first instance because of their achievements – what Salman Rushdie (who has attracted a fair amount of such attention himself, as well as a more lethal kind of ill will) has called 'the culture of denigration'. Of course, journalists have a right and duty to resist hype, and to subject reputations to constant scrutiny and reassessment; and nobody wants coverage of the arts to aspire to the condition of *Hello!* magazine. But sometimes the intention behind a good deal of reviewing, interviewing and commentary in this area seems to be to inflict pain rather than to preserve standards.

Some say that in the more caring ethos of Tony Blair's Britain, 'jugular journalism' (Mark Lawson's phrase) is in retreat. Certainly the death of Princess Diana, and the extraordinary wave of popular feeling it generated, provoked a good deal of uneasy introspection, and retrospective guilt, among journalists. Whether the effect will be long-lasting remains to be seen, but it has focused new attention on that problematic interface between private lives and public interest where my play is situated.

The action of the play takes place in the summer of 1997.

ACT ONE

Act One Scene One. Sunday morning.

*A spacious modernised cottage in Sussex. The interior of the
ground floor has been modified to make an open-plan living-room
with dining area (stage right) and sitting area (stage left) with
armchair, sofa, coffee table and* chaise-longue. *Kitchen off dining
area, with door. Door upstage leads to hall. The front door is out
of sight stage left and the stairs to the first floor are out of sight
stage right. There is a window in the wall of the living-room stage
left. Furnishings and decor are comfortable, lived-in, not opulent,
suggestive of literary and artistic occupants. There are a number
of modern ceramic objects – plates, bowls, vases and suchlike –
on display, which look as if they are the work of the same person.
Extensive bookshelves incorporate a hi-fi system. There is a
television set downstage. The dining-table is laid for breakfast,
including a Thermos coffee jug.* ELEANOR, *a good-looking woman
of about fifty, wearing a dressing-gown over a nightdress, is sitting
on the sofa, evidently having finished her breakfast, reading the
news section of the* Sunday Gazette, *a broadsheet, with two piles of
other Sunday newspapers at her feet, the smaller one consisting of
sections already read, the larger and neater one of sections waiting
to be read.* ADRIAN, *who is about the same age as* ELEANOR, *also
wearing a dressing-gown over pyjamas, is seated at the table,
inspecting various packets of cereals, reading the small print on
them carefully. A jet passenger plane passes overhead, fairly low.
(This sound recurs at the beginning of each scene.)* ELEANOR *drops
the* Gazette *news section on to the 'read' pile, and picks up the
Review.*

> ADRIAN
> Did you know that cornflakes are eighty-four per
> cent carbohydrates, of which eight per cent are
> sugars?

ELEANOR, *absorbed in her newspaper, does not answer.* ADRIAN
picks up another packet, and scrutinises it.

ADRIAN

All-bran is only forty-six per cent carbohydrates, but eighteen per cent of them are sugars. Is eighteen per cent of forty-six better or worse than eight per cent of eighty-four?

ELEANOR *does not answer.* ADRIAN *picks up another packet.*

ADRIAN

Shredded Wheat seems to be the best bet. Sixty-seven per cent carbohydrates of which less than one per cent are sugars. And no salt. (*Beat*) I suppose that's why it doesn't taste of anything much.

ADRIAN *puts a portion of Shredded Wheat into his bowl, and pours on milk.*

ADRIAN

What are you so engrossed in?

ELEANOR

'Top People's Holiday Reading'.

ADRIAN

I trust Tony Blair has taken *Ivanhoe* with him to Tuscany.

ELEANOR

He doesn't seem to be a contributor.

ADRIAN

Actually that *Desert Island Discs* was the only time I had serious doubts about voting for him. I mean, you might conceivably want to reread *The Heart of Midlothian* on a desert island, or *Old Mortality*, but *Ivanhoe* . . . (*Shakes his head*)

ELEANOR, *who has paid no attention to this speech, turns over a page.*

ADRIAN

Anything else of interest in the cultural pages?

ELEANOR

A new British film is causing a stir in America. It's about male strippers in Sheffield.

ADRIAN
I can't see it catching on here.

ELEANOR
Damien Hirst is exhibiting a decapitated art critic in a tank of formaldehyde . . . Oh no, that's a joke.

ADRIAN
It's so hard to tell the difference these days.

ELEANOR
And there's a row brewing over the Royal Opera House.

ADRIAN
It all sounds reassuringly familiar.

ELEANOR *puts down the* Gazette *Review and picks up the news section of the* Sunday Sentinel.

ADRIAN
What's the front page news?

ELEANOR
All boring. Mostly about Diana's holiday with Dodi Fayed.

ADRIAN
But it was *last* Sunday, too.

ELEANOR
It's the ultimate silly season story. One of the tabloids has paid a quarter of a million for pictures of them kissing on his yacht.

ADRIAN
You could get quite a good Picasso for that.

ELEANOR*'s eyes widen as she glances at the foot of the page.*

ELEANOR
Good God!

ADRIAN
What's the matter?

> ELEANOR
> I don't believe it.

She drops the news section and searches through the pile of unread newspaper sections.

> ADRIAN
> What has happened to cause this amazement, he asked himself. Has Jeffrey Archer renounced his peerage? Has Richard Branson travelled on one of his own trains? Has—

> ELEANOR
> It says there's an interview with Sam in the *Sentinel* Review. By Fanny Tarrant.

> ADRIAN
> Oh, yes.

> ELEANOR (*looks at him in surprise*)
> You knew about it?

> ADRIAN
> Well, sort of.

> ELEANOR
> But we haven't been in touch with Sam for weeks. Months.

> ADRIAN
> The Tarrant woman called me up about it.

> ELEANOR
> You didn't tell me.

> ADRIAN
> I forgot. You were out, I think.

ELEANOR *resumes searching for the Review.*

> ELEANOR
> What did she want?

> ADRIAN
> Background about Sam.

ELEANOR
I hope you didn't give her any.

ADRIAN
I told her I wouldn't discuss my oldest friend behind his back.

ELEANOR
I should think not, especially with Fanny Tarrant. She eats men like Sam for breakfast. (*She pulls the* Sentinel *Review from the pile*)

ADRIAN *looks at a spoonful of Shredded Wheat halfway to his mouth.*

ADRIAN
Well, there's not a lot of sugar in Sam.

ELEANOR *riffles through paper.*

ELEANOR
Sir Robert Digby-Sissons wept when he read what Fanny Tarrant wrote about him.

ADRIAN
How do you know?

ELEANOR
It said so in another paper. Here it is. God, what a ridiculous photograph. I fear the worst. Look!

ELEANOR *holds open the paper for* ADRIAN *to see.*

ADRIAN
What's the matter with it?

ELEANOR
He's wearing riding boots. He doesn't ride. He doesn't even own a horse.

ADRIAN
They're not riding boots, they're cowboy boots. He wears them on his trail bike.

ELEANOR
Trail bike! When is he going to grow up? Anyway,

he isn't on a motorbike in the picture, he's sitting
in front of his computer, and a right wally he looks
too, in cowboy boots. (*She begins reading the article*)
Oh dear. Oh dear. Listen to this (*Reads aloud*):
'Samuel Sharp has done pretty well for the son of a
tobacconist in darkest Deptford. He owns a manor
farm in Kent with a hundred acres of arable land
which he leases because he's too busy writing award-
winning TV screenplays to farm them. You can tell
he fancies himself in the agrarian role, though, by
the way he swaggers around his estate with his Ralph
Lauren jeans tucked into high-heeled cowboy boots.
He can use the heels, actually, being a little short
in the shank. Stature is a sensitive point with him.
"Whatever you do, don't ask Sam about his height,"
said a friend, "or his toupee." I didn't know he wore
a toupee.' Some friend! (*To* ADRIAN) Was that you?

ADRIAN
Certainly not. Where's the low-sugar marmalade?

ELEANOR
We've run out. (ADRIAN *tuts and shakes his head
reproachfully.* ELEANOR *reads aloud:*) 'I went to
see Samuel Sharp wondering why he had been so
unlucky in matrimony. I left thinking I knew the
answer: the man's insufferable vanity.'

ELEANOR *looks at* ADRIAN *for a reaction. He is spreading
marmalade thinly on a slice of toast.*

ADRIAN
A bit harsh.

ELEANOR
Harsh! It's vicious. (*She continues reading*) 'The
heroine of Samuel Sharp's latest TV film, *Darkness*,
is described in the BBC's publicity handout as a
"nymphomaniac". I asked him if he had ever met a
nymphomaniac. "Yes, no, well, it depends on what
you mean by a nymphomaniac," he stammered.
"I've known women who made it pretty obvious

that they'd, you know, if I gave them the slightest encouragement, but it's difficult to say whether it was nymphomania, exactly . . ." I think he was delicately hinting that it's difficult for a handsome chap like himself to know whether the readiness of casual female acquaintances to roll over onto their backs and open their knees is the effect of their temperament or his irresistible sex appeal.' (ELEANOR *lays down newspaper*) Sam's going to be devastated when he sees this.

ADRIAN
Well, he did ask for it, one might say.

ELEANOR
You're not very sympathetic to your best friend.

ADRIAN
I said 'oldest friend'.

ELEANOR
Who's your best friend, then?

ADRIAN (*thinks*)
You are.

ELEANOR
Apart from me.

ADRIAN (*thinks*)
I don't think I've got one. Sadly, it's not a concept that belongs to middle age.

Sound off of a car's tyres on gravel drive.

ELEANOR
Who can that be?

ADRIAN *goes to the window and peers out*

ADRIAN (*calmly*)
It's Sam.

ELEANOR (*not believing him*)
Ha, ha.

7

                        ADRIAN
        Is he not the owner of a green Range Rover,
        registration number SAM 1?

ELEANOR *goes to window, still holding the newspaper, and looks*
out. Sound off of car door slamming shut.

                        ELEANOR
        My God, it *is* Sam.

ELEANOR *makes for the door, stops, turns back and thrusts the*
newspaper into ADRIAN'*s hand.*

                        ELEANOR
        Here, hide this.

                        ADRIAN
        Why?

Doorbell chimes off.

                        ELEANOR
        He may not have seen it yet. Hide all the
        newspapers.

                        ADRIAN
        Where?

                        ELEANOR
        Anywhere.

ELEANOR *goes into hall and turns towards front door.* ADRIAN *looks*
around, slides paper under cushion on sofa. Sound of ELEANOR
unbolting front door and greeting SAM.

                        ELEANOR (*off*)
        Sam! What are you doing here at this time of the
        morning? Come in.

                        SAM (*off*)
        Thanks.

ADRIAN *pushes the other newspapers under the sofa just as* ELEANOR
returns, leading SAM. SAM *is about the same age as* ADRIAN, *but*

8

*shorter, and dresses younger, in smart casual clothes. He is carrying
a folded copy of the* Sunday Sentinel *Review.*

> ELEANOR (*to* ADRIAN)
> Adrian, it's Sam.

> ADRIAN (*pretends surprise*)
> Sam! What brings you here?

> SAM
> I'm flying to LA this morning, from Gatwick.
> Thought I'd drop in on my way.

> ELEANOR
> What a lovely surprise. Have you had breakfast?

> SAM
> As much as I could stomach.

> ELEANOR
> Would you like some coffee?

> SAM
> Thanks, that would be nice.

> ELEANOR (*picks up coffee pot*)
> I'll make a fresh pot.

> SAM
> No, don't bother. That will do fine. (*Holds up* Sentinel
> Review) Have you seen this?

> ELEANOR
> What is it?

> SAM
> Today's *Sentinel*. Did you read what that bitch
> Fanny Tarrant has written about me? (*He sits down
> on the sofa, feels the newspaper under the cushion, and
> pulls it out*) I see you have.

> ELEANOR
> I glanced at it.

> SAM (*to* ADRIAN)
> Did you?

ADRIAN
Ellie read out some bits to me.

SAM *looks reproachfully at* ELEANOR. *She hands him a cup of coffee.*

ELEANOR
Just the beginning.

SAM
Well, it doesn't get any better.

ADRIAN
How do you feel about it?

SAM
I feel as if I've been shat on from a great height by a bilious bird of prey.

ADRIAN
That's rather good. Did you just think of it?

SAM
It's a quotation.

ADRIAN
Is it? From what?

SAM
From my last series but one.

ADRIAN
Oh.

ELEANOR
Sam, what possessed you, to let that woman interview you? You must have read her stuff.

SAM (*evasively*)
I can't remember. There are so many of them, with their columns and their interviews . . .

ELEANOR
But she's famous.

SAM

No, *I'm* famous. She hasn't been around long
enough to be famous.

ELEANOR

Notorious, then. For being rude about people.

SAM

She rang me up one day, drooling over *The Bottom
Line*. She really seemed to love it.

ELEANOR

And you fell for that old ploy?

SAM

I gave her lunch, too. Prepared it myself: home-
made watercress soup, cold poached salmon with
mayonnaise – real mayonnaise, not that stuff like
Brylcreem out of a jar. And a bottle of Pouilly Fuissé
that cost a hundred and fifty quid a case.

ELEANOR

Poor Sam.

SAM *looks at* ADRIAN.

ADRIAN

It does seem ungrateful. After the mayonnaise and
everything.

SAM

I suppose you think it's funny?

ADRIAN

No, no. (SAM *stares suspiciously*. ADRIAN *shakes his
head vigorously*) No.

ELEANOR

Sam, I'm going to throw some clothes on. You can
stay a little while?

SAM

Half an hour or so.

ELEANOR

Oh, good. I won't be a minute. We haven't seen you
for ages.

SAM

I've been insanely busy lately. I haven't seen
anyone.

ADRIAN

Except Fanny Tarrant.

ELEANOR *goes out into hall, turning towards the stairs.*

SAM

That was work. Just because you've backed out of
the limelight, Adrian, you needn't feel superior to
those of us who still have to hang in there.

ADRIAN

'Hang in there'? I'm afraid your speech has been
corrupted by these meetings in Hollywood, Sam.

SAM

I've got a particularly important one on Tuesday.
I hope to God they don't take the *Sunday
Schadenfreude* at the studio.

ADRIAN

You can be sure someone will send it to them.

SAM

Thanks for cheering me up.

ADRIAN

It's the world we live in, Sam. Or, rather, the world
you live in.

SAM

What world is that?

ADRIAN

A world dominated by the media. The culture
of gossip.

SAM

The culture of envy, you mean. There are people in
this country who simply hate success. If you work
hard, make a name, make some money, they'll do
everything in their power to do you down.

ADRIAN

But you *put* yourself in their power, by agreeing to be interviewed by the likes of Fanny Tarrant.

SAM

It's easy to preach when you've never been asked.

ADRIAN

I have been asked.

SAM (*surprised*)

What, by Fanny Tarrant? (ADRIAN *nods*) When?

ADRIAN

A few weeks ago.

SAM

And what did you say?

ADRIAN

I said, no thanks.

SAM

Why did she want to interview you?

ADRIAN

I'm not a completely forgotten writer, you know.

SAM

Of course not, I didn't mean . . .

ADRIAN

The Hideaway is a set text at 'A' level.

SAM

And so it should be. But *The Hideaway* was published nearly twenty years ago. Sunday papers usually go for something a little more topical. What was Fanny Tarrant's hook?

ADRIAN

Hook?

SAM (*as if explaining to a child*)

Yes, hook. For example, my interview is hooked to the upcoming transmission of *Darkness*.

ADRIAN
Oh, I see.

SAM
But I doubt if Fanny Tarrant was proposing to
hang her interview with you on the *Paragon Book
of Cricket Writing*. That was your most recent
anthology, wasn't it?

ADRIAN
No, it was *Wills and Testaments* . . . I don't know
why she wanted to interview me. It was just an
aside. She actually called to ask me some questions
about *you*.

SAM
I hope you didn't tell her anything.

ADRIAN
Of course not.

SAM
Well, somebody did. Somebody told her that I
. . . (*Stops*)

ADRIAN
Wear a toupee? (SAM *looks accusingly at him*) It
wasn't me!

SAM
If I could get my hands on her now, I'd strangle
the bitch.

ADRIAN
Why allow yourself to get so angry? That's
exactly what she wants. Deny her the satisfaction.
Laugh it off.

SAM
You wouldn't say that if you'd read the whole thing.

ADRIAN
Let me have a look.

ADRIAN *takes the paper, which is already folded back at the*

appropriate page, from SAM *and begins to read silently. After a few
moments he sniggers.*

ADRIAN
She's quite witty, isn't she?

SAM (*coldly*)
D'you think so?

ADRIAN (*continues to scan article*)
What's she like?

SAM
Fanciable but frigid. Good legs. I never got a proper
look at her tits, she kept her jacket on.

ADRIAN
I meant, what social type?

SAM
Oh . . . Essex girl with attitude. Went to Basildon
Comprehensive and read English at Cambridge. She
calls herself a post-feminist.

ADRIAN
So she does. (*Reads*) 'Samuel Sharp said, "I never
did understand that word." I said it meant that I'd
assimilated feminism without being obsessed by it.
He said, with a roguish smile, "Oh, then I'm a post-
feminist too." I said that the treatment of women in
his screenplays made that hard to believe. He bridled
somewhat, and said, "What do you mean?" I said
that I'd been looking at videos of all his TV films
and series, and without exception they all featured
scenes in which women were naked and men were
clothed. The striptease joint in *The Bottom Line*, the
artist's studio in *Brush Stroke*, the operating theatre
in *Fever Chart*, the Peeping Tom scene in *Happy
Returns*, the rape scene in *Shooting the Rapids*, the
slave-market scene in *Dr Livingstone, I Presume*.' (*To*
SAM) She certainly did her homework, didn't she?

SAM
She's picking out one tiny component of my work
and blowing it up out of all proportion.

ADRIAN (*reads*)
'And in his latest film, *Darkness*, which he directed
himself—' (*To* SAM) Is that wise, directing yourself?

SAM
Who understands my work better?

ADRIAN *stares at* SAM *for a moment, lost for words, then continues
reading aloud.*

ADRIAN
'. . . there's a long scene in which a young woman
walks around her apartment naked, preparing a meal
for a man who's fully clothed.'

SAM
But that's because she thinks the guy is blind!

ADRIAN (*reads*)
'"But that's because she thinks he's blind!" Samuel
Sharp exclaimed. As if that made it all right. I
said, "But *we* know he *isn't* blind. Doesn't that just
intensify the voyeuristic thrill? Isn't it the schoolboy
fantasy of being invisible in the girls' locker
room? Aren't you exploiting the actors to achieve
that end?"'

SAM
You see what I mean. It's sheer undiluted malice.

SAM *stretches out his hand for the paper.* ADRIAN *holds on to it.*

ADRIAN
'He said, "Actors may have to bare their bums
occasionally. I bare my soul every time I put finger
to keyboard."' (*To* SAM) Did you really say that?

SAM (*defensively*)
Possibly. But the rest is a tissue of lies and
distortions. I'm going to write a letter to the paper.

ADRIAN
Write it, by all means, but don't post it.

SAM
Why not?

ADRIAN

You'll only make yourself look weak.

SAM

I've got to do something.

ADRIAN (*thinks*)

You could put Fanny Tarrant into your next television series, thinly disguised as a raving nymphomaniac.

SAM

It would never get past the lawyers.

ADRIAN

You'll just have to grin and bear it, then.

SAM

It would be more effective if the counter–attack came from somebody else . . .

Pause. SAM *looks thoughtfully at* ADRIAN.

ADRIAN

You want *me* to write a letter to the *Sentinel*?

SAM

No, I've got a better idea. Suppose you agree to be interviewed by Fanny Tarrant . . .

ADRIAN

Sounds like a very bad idea to me.

SAM

Remember how we hoaxed that reporter from the local rag in 'sixty-eight? During the great sit-in?

ADRIAN

How could I forget? (*Quotes*) 'The Student Revolutionary Council demands appointment of professors by democratically elected committees representing all sections of the university.'

SAM (*reminding* ADRIAN)

'Including porters, tea-ladies and cleaning staff.'

ADRIAN
'We demand student self-assessment instead of exams.'

SAM
'Double beds for students cohabiting in University residences.'

ADRIAN
'Smoking of marijuana to be permitted in tutorials.'

SAM
And he wrote it all down like a lamb and went away and they printed it all over the front page of the *Post*.

They laugh reminiscently.

ADRIAN (*penny drops*)
You're not suggesting that I try to hoax Fanny Tarrant?

SAM
Why not?

ADRIAN
Pretend to be a wife-beating paedophile drug addict, you mean? And hope she'd be silly enough to print it?

SAM
Well, it needn't be quite as lurid as that.

ADRIAN (*shakes head*)
This woman isn't a provincial cub reporter, Sam. It wouldn't work.

SAM (*regretfully*)
No, you're probably right. (*He thinks*) Hang about . . . Suppose you give her a straight interview, but use the opportunity to write a piss-take profile of *her*, for one of the other papers?

ADRIAN
What?

SAM

We wouldn't have any trouble placing it. There are
lots of people who would like to see Fanny Tarrant
taken down a peg or two. I know someone on the
Chronicle who'd jump at it.

ADRIAN

Sam—

SAM

Turn the tables on the bitch! Interview her when
she thinks she's interviewing you! Dig into her
background. Find out what makes her tick. Why the
envy? Why the malice? Lay it all out. Give her some
of her own medicine.

ADRIAN

Wouldn't she be suspicious if I rang her up and said
I'd changed my mind?

SAM

You have no idea how arrogant these people are.
They think the whole world is just longing to be
interviewed by them.

ADRIAN

That wasn't the impression I gave her.

SAM

Then we'll get someone else to ring her up for you
. . . Your agent! The perfect alibi: you mentioned
her invitation casually to him and he talked you into
doing it.

ADRIAN

Of course Geoffrey would love to see my name in
the papers again, but—

SAM

There you are! You could do a wonderful piece.
Weave in all that stuff about the culture of gossip.
You'd enjoy it.

ADRIAN

There's just one drawback to your scheme.

SAM
What's that?

ADRIAN
I'd get stitched up by Fanny Tarrant in the process.

Pause.

SAM
Not necessarily.

ADRIAN
No?

SAM
No . . . She isn't always bitchy.

ADRIAN
Isn't she? I thought you couldn't remember whether
you'd read her stuff.

SAM
I saw a nice piece by her once, about somebody.
Who was it?

ADRIAN
Mother Teresa?

SAM
God, no, she was vicious about Mother Teresa . . .

ADRIAN (*surprised*)
Mother Teresa gave her an interview?

SAM
No, that was one of her Diary columns . . . She can't
bear the thought of somebody being genuinely good
and seriously famous.

ADRIAN
Well, that would leave me in the clear, certainly.

SAM
Look, these people dare not write knocking copy
all the time, otherwise nobody would ever speak to
them. Every now and again they do a sympathetic

interview just to keep the pot boiling. I bet she's got you lined up as her next Mr Nice Guy.

ADRIAN
Did you hope to fill that slot yourself?

This seems to be a shrewd guess.

SAM
If I did, I made a big mistake . . . Come on, Adrian. I'm your old mate. Do this for me. Please!

SAM *goes down theatrically on his knees.* ELEANOR, *dressed, comes in from the hall.*

ELEANOR
What's going on?

ADRIAN
Sam wants to take out a contract on Fanny Tarrant, with me as the hit man.

SAM *scrambles to his feet.*

SAM (*to* ELEANOR)
Well, when Adrian told me she's itching to interview him—

ELEANOR *is very surprised.*

ELEANOR (*to* ADRIAN)
Fanny Tarrant wants to interview *you?*

ADRIAN
She mentioned it when she rang me up about Sam.

SAM
The idea is—

ELEANOR (*to* ADRIAN)
But why?

ADRIAN
I don't know. She was probably just buttering me up.

SAM
The idea is, you see—

Act One Scene One

ADRIAN
Sam's idea is—

SAM
The idea is, Adrian agrees to be interviewed in order
to write a satirical profile of Fanny Tarrant – unknown
to her, of course. (ELEANOR *looks at* ADRIAN. *He shakes
his head*) I like it more the more I think about it. It
could be the start of a whole new genre. The worms
turn. The artists fight back. Christ knows it's time.
These young arseholes have had it all their way for
too long. Why should we always have to grit our teeth
and take it like good sports? Why shouldn't we hand it
out for a change? Artists of the world unite! We have
nothing to lose but our Queensberry rules.

ELEANOR (*dismissively*)
Don't be silly, Sam.

ADRIAN *moves towards the door.*

ELEANOR
Where are you going?

ADRIAN
To the loo, if I have your permission.

ELEANOR
Oh.

SAM *points to the* Sentinel *Review in his hand.*

SAM
Are you taking that with you?

ADRIAN
Something to read.

ADRIAN *goes out.*

SAM (*calls after him*)
Wipe your bottom on it!

ELEANOR
Sam, why get so upset? It's only a silly little article,
by a silly little journalist.

SAM

But everybody I know will read it. At this very
moment sniggers are rising like sacrificial smoke
from a thousand breakfast tables all across London
and the Home Counties.

SAM *picks up a pottery jug.*

SAM

This is nice. Did you make it?

ELEANOR

Yes.

SAM

Very nice . . . Is it for sale?

ELEANOR

Not to you, Sam. If you like it, have it as a present.

SAM

No way. Would a hundred be fair?

ELEANOR

Far too much.

SAM

I'll give you seventy-five. (*He takes out cheque book
and writes cheque*)

ELEANOR

That's very generous. I am selling the odd piece
now, actually. It's very satisfying.

SAM

Ellie, tell me, am I really such a shit as that bitch
makes out?

ELEANOR (*pretends to take thought*)

Well . . .

SAM

All right, so I'm a bit vain. But I have every reason
to be. Three BAFTAs, two Royal Television Society
Awards, one Emmy, one Silver Nymph—

23

ELEANOR
Silver Nymph?

SAM
From the Monte Carlo TV Festival, they give you a
silver nymph. One Golden Turd from Luxembourg
– at least, that's what it looked like. Here. (*Gives*
ELEANOR *the cheque*)

ELEANOR
Thank you, Sam.

SAM
And now I'm writing real movies, maybe I'll win
an Oscar.

ELEANOR
What's your film about?

SAM
Florence Nightingale.

ELEANOR
What do you know about Florence Nightingale?

SAM
More than the producers, which is the main thing.
Actually there is a script already. They want me to
do a rewrite.

ELEANOR
Will it have a nude scene?

SAM
You may mock, Ellie. But I shall get paid three
hundred thousand dollars for a month's work. And
have a house with pool in Beverly Hills to do it in.

ELEANOR
Goodness!

SAM (*consciously hamming*)
But what use is my success, when I have nobody
to share it with? I live all alone in my luxuriously
furnished farmhouse, wading from room to room

through the deep-pile carpet, listening to the ticking of the clocks, longing for the phone to ring.

ELEANOR
You just said you were too busy to come and see us.

SAM
I'm busy *and* lonely. And, well . . .

ELEANOR
What?

SAM
It's hard to say it, Ellie, but, frankly, it embarrasses me to meet Adrian now. You remember what it was like in the old days. He was writing his novels, I was writing my plays. We used to swap stories about how our work was going. Now I come here and babble on about my projects and he has sod-all to say in return. It's like serving at tennis to an opponent with no arms.

ELEANOR
He doesn't mind.

SAM
Well, I mind. It makes me seem . . . boastful.

ELEANOR (*ironically*)
Surely not, Sam.

SAM
He's stagnating. You're both stagnating.

ELEANOR
No we're not. I have my ceramics. Adrian has his anthologies.

SAM
You never go anywhere.

ELEANOR
We go for walks on the Downs. Or drive to the sea.

SAM
I don't mean walks and drives.

Act One Scene One

ELEANOR *begins to recover the papers from under the sofa and stack them tidily.*

> ELEANOR
> If you mean first nights, launch parties, Groucho's, that sort of thing—

> SAM
> Yes, I mean that sort of thing.

> ELEANOR
> We've lost interest.

> SAM
> Adrian may have lost interest. You haven't. Otherwise, why do you take all these Sunday papers?

> ELEANOR (*smiles*)
> *Touché.*

> SAM
> If you were married to me, you would be *in* them, not just reading them.

> ELEANOR
> This morning that doesn't seem such an inviting prospect.

> SAM
> Oh, yes. *Touché.* (*Gloomily*) The bitch.

Pause.

> SAM
> Why has Adrian stopped writing?

> ELEANOR
> He's just stopped writing fiction. Sort of retired from it.

> SAM
> I don't believe that. Writers don't retire. No one gives it up voluntarily.

> ELEANOR
> He still writes non-fiction.

SAM

You mean those anthologies? That's scissors-and-paste work.

ELEANOR

They have introductions.

SAM

Yes, they have introductions. Ellie, for Christ's sake, Adrian Ludlow was the white hope of the English novel once!

ELEANOR

Yes, well, that was a long time ago . . . Sam, I don't like discussing Adrian with you like this, behind his back.

SAM *moves closer to* ELEANOR *and attempts to put his arm round her waist.*

SAM (*half-jokingly*)

If we were lovers it would seem more natural.

ELEANOR *gracefully evades his embrace.*

ELEANOR

Are you trying to get even with Laura?

SAM

Laura's history. It was a mistake from the beginning.

ELEANOR

I always thought you were too old for her—

SAM

No, she was too young for me. But you're right. I need a mature woman.

ELEANOR

You should have stuck with Georgina.

SAM

Georgina should have stuck with me, you mean. I wonder if it was Georgina told that bitch about my — (*Stops in mid-sentence*)

ELEANOR

Toupee? (SAM *looks piqued*) Sorry, Sam. I didn't mean to tease you.

ELEANOR *gives* SAM *a conciliatory kiss on the cheek. He takes hold of her and gives her a kiss on the lips.* ELEANOR *half-responds, then breaks away.*

ELEANOR

No, Sam . . .

SAM

Why not?

ELEANOR

You're just using me to salve your wounded ego.

SAM

No I'm not.

ELEANOR

No other woman being available on a Sunday morning.

SAM

Ellie, not a day goes by but I don't wish you'd married me instead of Adrian.

ELEANOR

Liar.

SAM

It's true.

ELEANOR

Adrian asked me, you didn't.

SAM

But he cheated. We didn't believe in marriage in those days, remember?

ELEANOR

I try not to.

SAM

We were going to start a commune.

ELEANOR
Hah! Some commune it would have been with two
writers in it.

SAM
But Adrian saw that secretly you yearned for the old
bourgeois certainties. I bet he even went down on his
knees, didn't he?

ELEANOR (*vehemently*)
Sam, I don't want to talk about it.

The conversation seems to have suddenly taken a turn SAM *hadn't
anticipated.*

ELEANOR
You know why.

ADRIAN *comes in from the hall in time to hear the last line. He
is dressed in tracksuit and trainers, with towel round his neck,
carrying the* Sentinel *Review.*

ADRIAN
Why what?

ELEANOR
Nothing.

To cover a certain embarrassment, ELEANOR *begins to put
soiled breakfast things on a tray.*

SAM (to *Adrian*)
Why are you wearing a tracksuit?

ADRIAN
I usually go for a little jog on Sunday mornings and
then have a sauna. Followed by—

SAM
Don't tell me you still poach yourself in that foetid
garden shed?

ADRIAN
The facilities are much improved since you last saw
them. It's a pity you haven't got time to join me.

29

SAM
No thank you.

ADRIAN
It would do you good. Sweat Fanny Tarrant's
poisons out of your system.

SAM
Saunas give me a rash.

ELEANOR
Are you sure you wouldn't like some fresh coffee,
Sam?

SAM
Some juice would be lovely, if you've got it.

ELEANOR
Right.

ELEANOR *takes tray out to kitchen.*

ADRIAN
Well, I finished it. (*He puts the* Sentinel *Review down*)

SAM
I don't blame you for being leery of her. But if you
published your piece at the same time as hers, it
would take the wind out of her sails.

ADRIAN
I'm not afraid of Fanny Tarrant.

SAM (*not paying attention*)
Or better still, *before* hers. Then the *Sentinel* might
not run her piece on you at all. And anyway—

ADRIAN
Sam—

SAM
Anyway, the sales of your backlist will go up,
whatever she says about you.

ADRIAN
My sales are not bad, actually. *The Hideaway* is—

SAM

An 'A' level set text. Yes, you said. But that's not
going to make you rich, Adrian. Nor is another
Paragon Book of Boring Crap. What you need is
a telly serial, and a tie-in paperback reissue. I tell
you what: I'll put *The Hideaway* up to the BBC for
serialisation.

ADRIAN

They turned it down years ago.

SAM

Yes, but this time *I'd* be offering to do the script.

ADRIAN

You could have offered before now.

SAM

Well, I suppose I could've, but, you know how it is.
I've been so busy . . .

ADRIAN

Sam, you don't have to try and bribe me.

SAM

I'm not! I'm not. Look, I'll pitch *The Hideaway*
to the Beeb as soon as I get back from the States.
I'll do it whether you go through with this Fanny
Tarrant sting or not, honest. All I ask is that you
think about it. (*Looks at watch*) Christ, I must get
going. Just think about it, OK?

ADRIAN

I've already thought about it. I'll do it.

SAM

What?

ADRIAN

I've been trying to tell you. I decided while I was in
the loo. I'll do it.

ELEANOR *appears at the kitchen door with jug of orange juice and
glasses on a tray in time to hear this, and stops.*

> SAM (*wrong-footed*)
> Oh. Well, great!

> ELEANOR
> Do what?

ELEANOR *looks across the room at* ADRIAN. ADRIAN *does not respond.* SAM *looks from one to the other.*

> SAM
> I must dash, Ellie. Sorry about the juice. (*To* ADRIAN) I'll phone Peter Reeves at the *Chronicle* and tell him to get in touch with you. I'll see myself out. *Ciao.*

SAM *goes out.*

> ELEANOR
> Do what?

ADRIAN *smiles blandly, but does not reply.* SAM *reappears in the doorway.*

> SAM (*to* ADRIAN)
> The thing is, to find her weak point, her Achilles heel, her guilty secret.

> ADRIAN
> Perhaps she hasn't got one.

> SAM
> Everybody's got one.

Pause. This remark seems to have more implications, or applications, than SAM *intended.*

> SAM (*to* ELEANOR)
> Well . . . 'Bye, Ellie. I'll collect the pot when I get back.

> ELEANOR
> Sam!

> SAM
> Sorry, must rush.

He goes. Sound of front door slamming.

ELEANOR

You don't mean to say that you've agreed to that crazy idea? You're not going to let Fanny Tarrant interview you?

ADRIAN

If she really wants to.

ELEANOR

Are you mad?

ADRIAN

I don't think so.

ELEANOR

You saw what she did to Sam. How will you feel if she does it to you?

ADRIAN

It won't bother me.

ELEANOR

Oh? What makes you so confident?

ADRIAN

Because I'm not competing any more. I'm outside the game.

ELEANOR

What game?

ADRIAN

The fame game. I've got nothing to lose. Unlike Sam, I don't *care* what Fanny Tarrant says about me.

ELEANOR

So you think . . . Anyway, why should you fight Sam's battles for him?

ADRIAN

He says he'll adapt *The Hideaway* for the BBC.

ELEANOR

Nothing will come of it.

ADRIAN
I know.

ELEANOR
So why are you doing this?

ADRIAN
There'll be a fee, if it comes off . . . The *Chronicle*
pays quite well, I believe. You could get that
new kiln.

ELEANOR (*dismissive gesture*)
Why, Adrian?

ADRIAN *hesitates*.

ADRIAN
Well, you know I've been a bit stuck for a theme for
my next anthology?

ELEANOR
No, I didn't.

ADRIAN
Well, I have. While I was in the loo just now, I
had an idea: the Paragon Book of Interviews. From
classical times to the present day. Starting with
Socrates and Ion of Ephesus, and ending with Fanny
Tarrant and the editor.

ELEANOR *is only half-convinced*.

ELEANOR
You'd reprint her interview with you?

ADRIAN
It would be a rather novel twist, don't you think?

ELEANOR
Supposing it was as nasty as her piece about Sam?

ADRIAN
That would make it representative.

ELEANOR
Supposing she refused permission?

ADRIAN

Then I might reprint my piece about her. In any
case, the experience would be very useful when I
write my introduction.

ELEANOR

I know what this is about! You're trying to recover
your lost youth.

ADRIAN

Ah, I sense a little psychoanalysis in the offing. Let
me adopt a suitable posture.

ADRIAN *lies on the* chaise-longue *in the posture of a psychoanalyst's
patient.*

ELEANOR

You're trying to get back to that golden time when
you and Sam were best friends, not just old friends.
When you both had the world before you.

ADRIAN

Go on.

ELEANOR

And you were both on equal terms. Or perhaps you
had the edge. Most people thought so. But now that
Sam is so successful, and you're . . .

ADRIAN

A failure?

ELEANOR

I was going to say, semi-retired. Call it what you
like . . . it's affected your relationship. You imagine
that by doing this favour for Sam you'll get back on
terms with him.

ADRIAN (*gets up*)

An ingenious theory. I must admit I feel a tingle of
anticipation about this project that I haven't felt for a
very long time. I never had much fun writing novels.

ELEANOR

You needn't tell me.

35

Act One Scene Two

ADRIAN (*glances at watch*)
I'd better go for my jog now, or there won't be time for a sauna before lunch.

ELEANOR
You'll regret it.

ADRIAN
No, I won't. I promise.

ADRIAN *goes out.* ELEANOR *is left alone. Her expression is troubled, apprehensive.*

Blackout.

Act One Scene Two. Eight days later, late morning.

ADRIAN *is alone in the living-room area of the cottage. He is dressed in well-worn casual clothes. On the table is a tray with the Thermos coffee jug, two cups and saucers, milk and sugar. Classical music – Bach or Handel – is playing on the hi-fi. Some of the furniture appears to have been moved around since we last saw it, and* ADRIAN *is engaged in moving the pieces back to their original positions. As he is replacing a picture on the wall, the doorbell rings.* ADRIAN *leaves the picture slightly askew, goes to the hi-fi, and touches a control. The music stops. He touches a couple of other controls. The lights on the system are still on. He goes into the front hall. Muffled exchange of greetings off. Then* ADRIAN *reappears with* FANNY, *a good-looking young woman in her late twenties, smartly dressed, carrying a slimline leather briefcase. She speaks with an accent that might be described as 'educated Estuary'.*

FANNY
Was that your wife who drove out of the gate as my taxi was trying to get in?

ADRIAN
In a white Peugeot?

FANNY
Yes.

ADRIAN
Yes. She's gone to visit her niece in East Grinstead.

FANNY
Pity. I was hoping to meet her.

ADRIAN
That was what she wanted to avoid.

FANNY
Oh, why is that?

ADRIAN
She reads your articles. Won't you sit down? (ADRIAN
gestures to a chair. FANNY *sits down*) She particularly
remembers the one about that art historian – Sir
somebody double-barrelled.

FANNY
Sir Robert Digby-Sisson.

ADRIAN
That's the chap. You commented adversely on Lady
Digby-Sisson's fingernails.

FANNY
Does your wife bite her fingernails?

ADRIAN
No, she just didn't want to risk appearing in your
article in some similarly disparaging aside.

FANNY
It sounds as if she doesn't approve of your doing this
interview.

ADRIAN
No, she doesn't.

FANNY *opens her briefcase and takes out a small Sony audio cassette
recorder which she places on a coffee table.*

FANNY

You don't mind if I record the interview?

ADRIAN

Not at all. As long as you don't mind my recording
it too.

FANNY

By all means. (*She checks that her tape-recorder has a
cassette in it and switches it on*) D'you want to set up
your tape-recorder?

ADRIAN (*gestures to hi-fi system*)

It's already on. It has a very sensitive microphone.
Voice-activated. I hope yours is as good. I tend to
move about when I talk.

FANNY

It's state-of-the-art. Why do you want to record our
conversation?

ADRIAN

To settle any disputes that might arise about
what I said.

FANNY

Fair enough. (*She takes a notebook and ballpoint pen
out of her briefcase, and looks round the room*) This is
nice. Have you been here long?

ADRIAN

It used to be our weekend retreat, but it was smaller
then. When we decided to move out of London, we
bought the adjoining cottage and knocked through
the party wall.

FANNY *makes shorthand notes on the furnishings etc.*

FANNY

You've been married quite a long time, haven't you?

ADRIAN

Yes.

FANNY

And you have two sons.

ADRIAN

They're grown up now – flown the nest. Are you married yourself?

FANNY

No.

ADRIAN

But you must have a . . . what's the approved term nowadays?

FANNY

Partner.

ADRIAN

Ah, yes. What's his name?

FANNY

Creighton.

ADRIAN

Spelled . . . ?

FANNY

C, r, e, i, g, h, t, o, n. Why do you ask?

ADRIAN

And what does Mr Creighton do—

FANNY

Creighton is his first name.

ADRIAN

Really? You mean, he was christened 'Creighton'?

FANNY

I'm not sure he was ever christened.

ADRIAN

Oh. A heathen, eh?

FANNY

There are quite a lot of them about, you know. Would you describe yourself as a Christian?

ADRIAN

Well, I attend the parish church at Christmas,

harvest festival, that sort of thing. I contribute to
the roofing fund. I believe in the Church of England
as an institution. I'm not sure about the doctrine. I
don't think the vicar is, either, as a matter of fact.
And yourself?

FANNY

I was brought up as a Catholic, but I haven't been to
church for years.

ADRIAN

How did you lose your faith?

FANNY

Look, this is going to take a very long time if you
keep asking *me* questions.

ADRIAN (*smiles sweetly*)
I've got all day.

Beat.

FANNY

All right. So have I. But what about Mrs Ludlow?

ADRIAN

She won't be back till this evening.

FANNY

I see. By the way, did everything go all right with
Freddy?

ADRIAN

Freddy?

FANNY

The photographer.

ADRIAN

Oh, yes. Fine, I think. Funny business though, isn't
it, photography?

FANNY

What's funny about it?

ADRIAN

Well, they come into your house, move all your

furniture about—

ADRIAN *notices that the picture on the wall is askew, and goes to straighten it.*

ADRIAN
Set up their lights and tripods and umbrellas and circus hoops all over the place—

FANNY
Circus hoops?

ADRIAN
Those folding things for reflecting light. Then they make you twist yourself into the most artificial postures and talk to you all the time like a barber, and keep telling you not to look so serious—

FANNY
Did Freddy tell you not to look so serious?

ADRIAN
No, but they usually do. I mean, they usually did in the days when I was photographed for book jackets.

FANNY
Freddy doesn't meddle with his subjects' natural expressions. That's why he's a first-class portrait photographer.

ADRIAN
Pretty extravagant with film, though, isn't he? He must have used at least three rolls.

FANNY
I think the paper can afford it.

ADRIAN
Yes. But why take so many pictures of the same face?

FANNY
To find the one that tells you most about the

subject. People's expressions are always changing, but so subtly and so fast that you don't know what you've captured until you develop the film. That's why photographs are more revealing than real life.

ADRIAN

And interviews, are they more revealing than real life?

FANNY

Interviews *are* real life. Mine are, anyway.

ADRIAN

Oh, come!

FANNY

I invent nothing. That's why I use this. (*She indicates the tape-recorder*)

ADRIAN

But you won't report *everything* I say, will you? You'll leave out the less interesting bits.

FANNY

Obviously. Otherwise it would be far too long and very boring to read.

ADRIAN

But you falsify a conversation if you leave out any part of it: the dull bits, the hesitant bits, the repetitions, the silences.

FANNY

There haven't been any silences.

ADRIAN

There will be.

Pause.

FANNY

All right. I concede the point.

ADRIAN

What point?

FANNY
That the interview is not pure, unmediated reality.

ADRIAN
No indeed! it's a game.

FANNY
A game?

ADRIAN
A game for two players. The question is, what are
the rules, and how does one win? Or lose, as the
case may be. Coffee? Eleanor left us some in the
Thermos.

FANNY
Thanks.

ADRIAN *goes over to table and pours coffee.*

ADRIAN
How do you take it?

FANNY
Black. No sugar.

ADRIAN
Very wise.

ADRIAN *hands a cup of coffee to* FANNY.

FANNY
Actually, I don't see it as a game. The interview,
I mean. I see it as a transaction. A barter. The
interviewer gets copy. The interviewee gets publicity.

ADRIAN
But I don't want publicity.

FANNY
Why did you agree to be interviewed, then?

ADRIAN
Why did you want to interview me?

FANNY
I asked first.

43

ADRIAN

All right. I was curious.

FANNY

Curious about what?

ADRIAN

About why you want to interview me.

FANNY *acknowledges the move with a wry smile.*

ADRIAN

You usually interview celebrities. I haven't been a celebrity for years, if I ever was one. So why me?

FANNY

I'm curious too. About why you aren't a celebrity any more. Why you stopped writing, why you dropped out of the literary world.

ADRIAN

I still publish books.

FANNY

Yes, I know. The Paragon anthologies. Anybody could do them.

ADRIAN

Well, not quite anybody. You have to be able to read. You have to know where to look for things.

FANNY

You see, your fiction meant a great deal to me once.

ADRIAN

Really?

FANNY

I read *The Hideaway* when I was fifteen. It was the first time a modern novel really excited me. I still think it's the best treatment of adolescence in post-war British fiction.

ADRIAN

Well, thank you. Thank you very much. It's an 'A'level set text, you know.

FANNY

God, what a depressing thought.

ADRIAN

Why?

FANNY

Well, the whole point of *The Hideaway* for me was
that it wasn't a set text, it wasn't prep, it wasn't
examination fodder. It was something private, secret,
subversive.

ADRIAN

I know what you mean.

FANNY

Can't you stop them teaching it?

ADRIAN

I don't think I can. Anyway, the royalties come
in useful.

FANNY

There was a group of us at school, we were like a
secret society. We used to read *The Hideaway* aloud
and argue about it – not in a lit-crit way, but about
who we liked best – Maggie or Steve or Alex – and
about what would've happened to them after the
story ended. It was like a religion. *The Hideaway* was
our bible.

ADRIAN

Good Lord. How long did that last?

FANNY

A whole term. A summer term.

ADRIAN

Then in the holidays you read another book and
based a new religion on that?

FANNY

No, there was never another book like *The Hideaway*.
I've brought my much-thumbed copy for you to
sign, actually, if you wouldn't mind.

> ADRIAN
> Of course.

FANNY *takes an old paperback copy of* The Hideaway *from her briefcase and hands it to* ADRIAN. *He writes in the flyleaf.*

> ADRIAN
> You were at a boarding-school, then?

> FANNY
> How did you guess?

> ADRIAN
> You said 'prep' rather than 'homework'.

> FANNY
> Ah.

ADRIAN *closes the book and hands it back to* FANNY, *who glances at the inscription and puts it in her briefcase.*

> FANNY
> Thanks.

> ADRIAN
> I thought you went to a comprehensive school in Basildon.

> FANNY
> Who told you that?

> ADRIAN
> Sam Sharp.

> FANNY
> I was wondering when his name would crop up. The trouble with Mr Sharp is that he doesn't listen to what anybody says to him. What I actually said was, that I *wished* I'd gone to a comprehensive school in Basildon.

> ADRIAN
> Why?

> FANNY
> It would have been a better preparation for

journalism than a convent boarding-school in Hampshire. Could we get back to you? Why did you stop writing fiction?

ADRIAN

I decided that my *oeuvre* was complete. That I had nothing more to say.

FANNY

Just like that?

ADRIAN

Just like that.

FANNY

Didn't it worry you?

ADRIAN

For a while. Then I began to enjoy it.

FANNY

How?

ADRIAN

It's like when you run out of petrol and your car stops. At first it's annoying, but after a while you come to appreciate the silence and tranquillity. You hear things you never heard before, because they were drowned by the noise of the engine. You see things that previously flashed by in a blur.

FANNY

Have you ever actually run out of petrol?

ADRIAN

Since you ask, no.

FANNY

I thought so.

ADRIAN

It was a metaphor.

FANNY

Doesn't it bother you, when you see your contemporaries still writing and publishing?

ADRIAN

On the contrary. There are too many writers around
who have nothing more to say, but insist on saying it
again and again, in book after book, year after year.

FANNY

Which writers are you thinking of?

ADRIAN

The same ones that you're thinking of.

FANNY

I can't believe you gave it up so easily.

ADRIAN

You mean, how could I give up all those long,
solitary hours spent staring at a blank page, or
gaping out of the window, gnawing the end of a
ballpoint, trying to create something out of nothing,
to will creatures with no previous existence into
being, to give them names, parents, education,
clothes, possessions, to have to decide whether they
have blue eyes or brown, straight hair or curly hair
or no hair – God, the tedium of it. And then the
grinding, ball-breaking effort of forcing it all into
words, fresh-seeming words, words that don't sound
as if you bought them second-hand as a job-lot. And
then having to set the characters moving, behaving,
interacting with each other in ways that will seem
simultaneously (*he ticks off the epithets on his fingers*):
interesting, plausible, surprising, funny and moving.
It's like playing chess in three dimensions. It's
absolute hell. Would *you* miss it?

FANNY

I'd miss the end result. The satisfaction of having
created something permanent. The effect you have
on other people.

ADRIAN

But you don't know, most of the time, what the
effect is. Writing novels is like putting messages into

bottle after bottle and tossing them into the sea on
the outgoing tide without any idea of where they'll
be washed up or how they will be interpreted. (*Beat*)
I *have* done that with bottles, by the way.

FANNY
What about reviews?

ADRIAN (*after a momentary hesitation*)
What indeed.

FANNY
Don't they give you some feedback?

ADRIAN
They tell you a lot about the reviewer. Not much
about your book.

FANNY
My first job in journalism was writing film reviews,
for a listings magazine.

ADRIAN
Were they as cruel as your interviews?

FANNY (*laughs dismissively*)
'Cruel'?

ADRIAN
Sir Robert Digby-Sissons thought you were cruel.
According to a rival journal, he wept on reading your
interview with him.

FANNY
He wept while he was *giving* the interview. He's
a big cry-baby. Tears gush from his eyes at the
slightest pretext. When he wasn't blubbing into his
handkerchief, he was trying to grope me.

ADRIAN
You didn't mention that in your article.

FANNY
I did, but it was cut. The lawyers were nervous
because I didn't have a witness. This thing (FANNY

indicates recorder) doesn't pick up the sound of a knee being squeezed.

ADRIAN
You were cruel to my friend Sam Sharp, too. He was very hurt.

FANNY
He'll survive.

ADRIAN
Yes, I dare say he will.

FANNY
Though I *was* a little surprised when you agreed to see me just after that piece appeared. I thought it might be a trap.

ADRIAN (*startled*)
Trap? What kind of trap?

FANNY
I thought perhaps Mr Sharp might be lurking in the house somewhere.

ADRIAN (*relieved laugh*)
No, Sam's in Los Angeles. But what did you think he would do? Assault you?

FANNY
It has been known.

ADRIAN
Really?

FANNY
You know Brett Daniel?

ADRIAN
The actor.

FANNY
The week after I published my interview with him he deliberately spilled a glass of red wine down the front of my dress at a first-night party. Then he followed

it with a white-wine chaser on the grounds that it
would take the stain out.

ADRIAN

Well, that does work, actually . . . Did you sue him?

FANNY

I sent him a whopping bill for a new dress. But he
told all his cronies it was worth every penny.

ADRIAN

You didn't think that Sam was going to leap out at
you here, flinging glasses of wine, did you?

FANNY

I thought he might leap out flinging insults.

ADRIAN

Doesn't it bother you, knowing that most of the
people you've interviewed hate you afterwards?

FANNY (*shrugs*)

It's all part of the job.

ADRIAN

It's a funny sort of job, though, isn't it? Character-
assassination, I mean.

FANNY

Are you trying to wind me up?

ADRIAN

No, no. But you must admit, your pieces are usually
pretty destructive. Isn't that what your readers expect
of you?

FANNY

They expect good journalism, and I hope I give
it to them. What do you think about the younger
generation of British novelists?

ADRIAN

I try not to think of them. But you're not telling
me, are you, that all those readers would be turning
eagerly to your page if you were billed as 'Fanny
Tarrant – Britain's Kindest Interviewer'?

FANNY

No, I'm not telling you that. I'm trying, with some
difficulty, to interview you.

ADRIAN

Your readers wouldn't stoop to reading about the
bonking escapades of footballers and pop stars in
the tabloids. But you give them the same kind of
pleasure in a more refined form, by making the great
and the good look silly.

FANNY

They do it unassisted. I just report it.

ADRIAN

Tell me, when you've written one of your really
nasty pieces, like the one on Sam—

FANNY

Oh, I can be much nastier than that.

ADRIAN

I don't doubt it. (*In what follows he maintains a tone
of detached curiosity*) But when you've written a piece
like that, and it's printed, do you imagine the victim
reading it? I mean, do you imagine poor old Sam,
say, getting up on Sunday morning, and padding
down the hall in his dressing-gown and slippers, and
picking up the *Sunday Sentinel* off the doormat, and
taking it into the kitchen to read with his first cup
of tea, and riffling through the pages of the Review
section to find your interview, and smiling as he
sees Freddy's full-page colour photo of him sitting
at his Apple Mac, and then starting to read the text,
and the sudden fading of his smile as he comes to
the first sneer, and then the thumping of his heart,
the spasm in the gut, the rush of adrenalin to the
bloodstream, as it dawns on him that the piece is *all*
sneers, that he has been well and truly stitched up.
I mean, do you imagine all that? Does it give you a
kick? Is that why you do this job?

FANNY *for once looks slightly rattled.*

FANNY
Could we get back to me asking the questions?

ADRIAN
Why?

FANNY
It's customary. The interviewer asks the questions and the interviewee answers them.

ADRIAN
That's why the interview is such an artificial form. It isn't a real dialogue. It's an interrogation.

FANNY
Well, interrogation has its uses.

ADRIAN
Such as what?

FANNY
Such as uncovering the truth.

ADRIAN
Oh, the truth . . . Did it never occur to you that my questions might reveal more than my answers?

FANNY
I prefer to stick to my own agenda, thanks.

ADRIAN
So you won't quote the question I just asked you?

FANNY
What question?

ADRIAN
Does it give you a kick to imagine your victims' pain?

FANNY (*irritably*)
I've no idea what I'm going to quote, yet.

ADRIAN
I suppose you have to listen to the whole tape first.

FANNY
I have a transcript made.

53

ADRIAN

And then you edit it on a word-processor? Or do you
write the first draft in longhand?

FANNY

You *are* winding me up, aren't you?

ADRIAN

No! No.

FANNY

That's straight out of the handbook for intellectually
challenged journalists, *One Hundred Boring Questions
to Ask an Author*. 'Do you write something every
day? Do you write with a fountain pen or on a
computer? Do you work out the whole story before
you start?'

ADRIAN (*a smile of recognition*)

'Are your novels autobiographical?'

FANNY

No, that's not a boring question.

ADRIAN

Well, I always used to give a boring answer.
'My novels are a mixture of personal experience,
observation of other people, and imagination. I like
to think that my readers won't be able to tell which
is which, and sometimes I'm not too sure myself.'

FANNY (*making a note*)

That's not a boring answer, either, actually.

ADRIAN

Why do you make notes if you've got a tape-
recorder? Belt and braces?

FANNY

The machine records your words. The notebook my
interpretations.

ADRIAN

Ah. (*He extends his hand*) Can I have a look?

FANNY

No. What's your earliest memory?

ADRIAN

My earliest memory . . . Hmm . . . What about some
lunch first?

FANNY

Lunch?

ADRIAN

Yes. Ellie left us some cold cuts and salad in the
fridge. And I could open a tin of soup.

FANNY

I don't usually eat lunch. But if you're hungry, I'll sit
down with you and nibble something.

ADRIAN

You don't eat lunch? But Sam was particularly
outraged that you abused him after eating the
delicious poached salmon he prepared for you.

FANNY

He ate most of it himself, actually. And drank
most of the wine. But please – if you want to eat –
go ahead.

ADRIAN

No, it doesn't matter. I often skip lunch myself, as
a matter of fact. I'm on a diet. I've become more
health-conscious since I gave up writing novels.

FANNY

That's interesting. Why?

ADRIAN

I suppose while I was pursuing literary immortality
I didn't think much about mortality. When I was a
novelist I had a pipe in my mouth all day, ate fried
breakfasts, drank the greater part of a bottle of wine
over dinner and hardly ever took any exercise. Now
I scrutinize every packet of food for E numbers,
eschew salt and sugar, measure my alcohol intake

in units, and jog every day. My only indulgence is
the sauna.

FANNY

I wouldn't describe a sauna as an indulgence.

ADRIAN

But the feeling afterwards – don't you find it
euphoric?

FANNY

The only time I tried it, I hated it.

ADRIAN

Where was that?

FANNY

Oh . . . some hotel 'leisure complex'.

ADRIAN

I expect you wore a swimming costume.

FANNY

Yes, of course.

ADRIAN

But you mustn't wear anything in the sauna! It
constricts the body, interferes with the sweating. It's
totally wrong.

FANNY

I didn't have any choice. It was a mixed sauna, right
next to the swimming-pool.

ADRIAN

I know. I bet it was full of people who squelched in
straight from the pool and sat there giving out clouds
of chlorinated steam . . . (FANNY *silently assents*) The
English really have no idea how to take a sauna. It's
enough to make you weep.

FANNY

How should you do it, then?

ADRIAN

First you take a warm shower. Then you dry off.

Then you bathe your feet and ankles in a warm
footbath. Then you enter the sauna, and sit or lie
on a bench – the higher it is the hotter it is – for ten
or fifteen minutes, until the sweat is breaking out
all over your body in beads; then you take a long
cold shower, or plunge into an icy lake if there's one
handy, then you wrap up in a bathrobe and relax
somewhere warm. There's nothing like it.

FANNY
Where do you go to do this?

ADRIAN
Into my back garden.

FANNY
You mean, you have your own sauna here?

ADRIAN
Yes. There's no lake, alas, but I've just built an
annexe with a shower and a cold plunge bath. Would
you like to see it? (*Gestures towards kitchen door*)

FANNY
Later perhaps.

ADRIAN *has an idea.*

ADRIAN
In fact . . . you could try it out. If I can't offer you
lunch, we could have a sauna instead.

FANNY (*incredulous*)
I beg your pardon?

ADRIAN
You could discover what a real sauna is like.

FANNY
No thank you.

ADRIAN
Why not?

FANNY
I don't usually interview people in the nude.

ADRIAN

Oh, one doesn't talk in the sauna. One communes silently with the heat. Afterwards one may talk.

FANNY *is silent, hesitating.*

ADRIAN

What are you afraid of? I would hardly risk being exposed in the *Sunday Sentinel* as a sex-maniac.

FANNY

I could make a good deal just out of this proposition, you know.

ADRIAN

Yes, you could. 'Adrian Ludlow invited me to try his private sauna as casually as one might offer a visitor a drink. He assured me I wouldn't need a swimming costume. I made my excuses and left.'

FANNY

I have no intention of leaving. I haven't finished my interview. I have a lot more questions to get through. (*She flips to the appropriate page of her notebook to check them*)

ADRIAN

Forget them.

FANNY

What?

ADRIAN

Tear them up. Let's start again, after a sauna. Not an interview. No set questions, and set answers. No disguises. No pretences. No games. Just a conversation, that takes its own course. What do you say?

FANNY *stares at* ADRIAN *as if trying to test his sincerity. He does not flinch.*

ADRIAN

I'll get you a bathrobe and towel, and show you where to change.

FANNY
What makes you think I've agreed?

ADRIAN
Haven't you?

FANNY *gets slowly to her feet.*

FANNY
I shall wrap the towel round me.

ADRIAN
Please yourself.

ADRIAN *goes to the kitchen door.* FANNY *lingers, switching off the tape-recorder and replacing it on the coffee table.* ADRIAN *stands at the kitchen door and looks at* FANNY.

ADRIAN
It's through here.

FANNY *walks coolly across the room and through the door, followed by* ADRIAN.

Blackout.

ACT TWO

Act Two Scene One. Forty minutes later.

The living-room of the cottage. FANNY *is lying on the sofa or*
chaise-longue, wrapped in a white towelling bathrobe. Her
tape-recorder is on the coffee table. Her hair is damp. Her feet are
bare, her eyes closed. A plane drones overhead. ADRIAN *comes in*
through the kitchen door, also wearing a white towelling bathrobe
and flip-flops, carrying a tray on which are a carton of orange juice
and two tumblers. He puts the tray down on the dining-table and
looks across at FANNY.

> ADRIAN
> How do you feel?

> FANNY
> Blissful. You've made a convert.

> ADRIAN
> Good.

Pause. ADRIAN *pours two glasses of orange juice.*

> FANNY
> You were quite right: it *is* much more comfortable
> when you're naked.

ADRIAN *smiles smugly.*

> ADRIAN
> You should have a drink now, to replace the fluid
> you lost. (*Hands her a glass of orange juice*)

> FANNY
> Thanks. How were you initiated yourself?

> ADRIAN
> At a Writers' Conference in the middle of Finland,

60

years ago. We were offered a choice of excursions:
a guided tour of the town, which looked about as
exciting as Milton Keynes, or a traditional smoke
sauna at a nearby lake. I chose the smoke sauna.

FANNY *switches on her tape-recorder*.

FANNY
What's that?

ADRIAN *goes close to* FANNY's *tape-recorder and announces the
topic with mock formality*.

ADRIAN
'A Smoke Sauna.' (*He continues in a normal tone of
voice*) They heat up the cabin with a wood fire and
let it fill with smoke. Then they open a trap door in
the roof just long enough to let the smoke escape,
but not the heat. When you go in, the whole place
smells deliciously of charred wood. The walls and
benches are covered with soot, and soon you are
too. The heat is tremendous. Sweat pours down your
body in rivulets.

FANNY
Making streaks in the soot.

ADRIAN
Exactly. There were all these famous writers
crammed into the cabin, haunch to haunch, looking
like savages in war-paint and smelling like barbecued
spare-ribs.

FANNY
Men and women together?

ADRIAN
No, the Finns were a bit prudish about that. The
ladies had a separate session, and we joined them for
beer and sausages later.

FANNY
It sounds like fun. Do you still go to these literary
junkets?

ADRIAN

I don't get invited any more.

FANNY

Being stuck in a country cottage under the
Gatwick flight paths must seem rather a dull life in
comparison.

ADRIAN

Not at all. It's a source of deep satisfaction to me
to reflect that I need never be part of those anxious
heaving masses in airport terminals again. Especially
in August.

FANNY

I know, I dread it. But I need my holiday.

ADRIAN

Where will that be?

FANNY

We're going to Turkey this year.

ADRIAN

It's surprising what you can do without, when
you try. Foreign holidays. New cars, new clothes.
Second houses. Getting and spending. It's no way to
live, really.

FANNY

You gave it all up when you gave up writing novels?

ADRIAN

That's right. It's called 'downshifting'. I read an
article about it. Or rather my wife read it out to me.

FANNY

Downshifting is quite a recent phenomenon.

ADRIAN

We were pioneers.

FANNY

And it started in America.

ADRIAN
No, it started here. Where do you live?

FANNY
I have a loft apartment in Clerkenwell.

ADRIAN
Which you share with Creighton?

FANNY
Yes.

ADRIAN
What does he do?

FANNY
He's a solicitor.

ADRIAN
So Creighton would be useful if one of your victims decided to sue you.

FANNY
I wish you wouldn't keep using that word.

ADRIAN
Creighton?

FANNY
Victims. People in public life must expect to get a few knocks. And other people enjoy seeing them get roughed up a bit.

ADRIAN
Ah! You admit that!

FANNY
Of course, it's human nature. When you read my piece about Sam Sharp, didn't you feel – as well as sympathy and outrage and all the other things a friend should feel – didn't you feel an undercurrent of delicious pleasure too? (ADRIAN *looks shifty*) The truth, now. 'No disguises, no pretences.'

Pause. FANNY *looks fixedly at* ADRIAN. *He meets her eyes.*

ADRIAN
All right! All right! I admit it.

FANNY *relaxes with a sigh of satisfaction.*

FANNY
Thank you.

ADRIAN
But what a terrible admission to make. How I hate
you for making me enjoy my friend's suffering.

FANNY
'Suffering' is rating Sam Sharp's bruised ego a
bit high.

ADRIAN
Don't you ever feel even the faintest spasm of
remorse when you see your articles in print?

FANNY
No.

ADRIAN (*holds her gaze*)
Truthfully, now.

FANNY
Why should I? I perform a valuable cultural
function.

ADRIAN
What is that?

FANNY
There's such a lot of hype nowadays, people confuse
success with real achievement. I remind them of the
difference.

ADRIAN
Does that entail making fun of their toupees and
cowboy boots?

FANNY
Sometimes it's the only way to penetrate their

64

conceit. Your friend Mr Sharp has a certain talent, but he doesn't work hard enough to perfect it. He writes too much, too fast. Why?

ADRIAN

He has an ex-wife to support. Two ex-wives.

FANNY

The more he earns, the more alimony he has to pay. It's not the need for money that makes him overproduce, it's laziness.

ADRIAN

Sam – *lazy*?

FANNY

Yes. By keeping the scripts spilling out of his computer, like cars rolling off a production line, he never gives himself time to assess the *quality* of what he's producing. That's where I come in. To question the nature of his 'success'. His next screenplay will be a little better than it otherwise might have been, because of the pinpricks I inflicted on his ego the other day.

ADRIAN

Hmm.

FANNY

You sound sceptical.

ADRIAN

Well, Sam and I go back a long way.

FANNY

You were at university together, weren't you?

ADRIAN

Yes. We were put in the same tutorial group in our first week. We became inseparable. Shared a flat together, edited a magazine together, wrote revue sketches together, got drunk together.

FANNY

There's a scene at the end of one of your novels,

65

where two undergraduates get drunk after their
finals . . .

ADRIAN
Salad Years. Yes, that was us. I came out of the
Union, and there was Sam, weaving about in the
middle of the campus, a bottle in his hand, looking
for me. We'd been drinking all afternoon, but had
got separated somehow. When he saw me, his face lit
up in delight, and he waved and tried to run towards
me. Only he was so drunk that his brain completely
screwed up the message it was trying to send to his
legs. Instead of carrying him towards me, they went
into reverse, and he started running backwards.
I could see his face filling with bewilderment and
alarm, as if he was being abducted by some invisible
force, but the harder he strained to run towards
me, the faster he ran backwards, until eventually he
overbalanced and fell flat on his back in a flowerbed.
It was the funniest thing I ever saw in my life. At
least, it seemed so then.

FANNY
Yes, it *is* funny in the book. But sad, too. The hero
feels it's a . . . kind of . . .

ADRIAN
Portent.

FANNY
Yes. Of how they're going to grow distant from each
other in the years to come.

ADRIAN
That's the benefit of hindsight. I didn't feel it at
the time.

FANNY
But that *was* what happened?

ADRIAN
It's inevitable. That sort of friendship belongs to
youth. It can't survive into adult life. Your lives

begin to diverge: you start separate careers, get
married, acquire responsibilities . . .

FANNY

Would you say there was a homosexual element in
your friendship at college?

ADRIAN

Good God, no!

FANNY

I don't mean anything overtly physical, but some
unconscious homoerotic attraction?

ADRIAN

Absolutely not. We were both in love with Ellie,
most of the time.

FANNY

Ellie?

ADRIAN (*already regretting this disclosure*)
My wife.

FANNY

Oh, I see. Oh, I *see*! So your wife is the girl in *Salad
Years* – what's her name, Fiona?

ADRIAN

No, no, Eleanor is a quite different sort of person.

FANNY

But she occupied the same position *vis-à-vis* you
and Sam as Fiona does with the two young men in
the novel?

ADRIAN (*hesitantly*)
Up to a point.

FANNY

In the book, they actually *share* Fiona for a time. She
sleeps with both of them.

ADRIAN

Look, I'd rather not discuss this any more, if you
don't mind.

FANNY

I thought this conversation was to take its own
course.

ADRIAN

As far as I'm concerned, yes. This concerns Ellie.

FANNY

So she did sleep with both of you?

ADRIAN

I didn't say that.

FANNY

You wouldn't be so defensive about it if she hadn't.

Pause, as ADRIAN *considers how to proceed.*

ADRIAN

No, I'm sorry.

FANNY

Off the record. (*She turns off her tape-recorder*)

ADRIAN

What use is it to you off the record?

FANNY

I told you, my interest is more than just professional.

ADRIAN

How do I know I can trust you?

FANNY

You can trust me.

Pause.

ADRIAN

All right. Sam and I wrote a revue for the Drama
Society in our second year, and Ellie turned up for
an audition. Sam and I fell for her at once, and she
took to us. We didn't want to fight over her, so we
got in the habit of going around all together, as a

68

threesome. People in our peer group couldn't quite work out what was going on between us. We enjoyed keeping them guessing.

FANNY

And what *was* going on?

ADRIAN

Nothing, sexually. We used to sit around smoking pot, and sometimes there would be a cuddling session *à trois*, but nothing more. Then one day Sam got a message that his father was seriously ill, and dashed home. Ellie and I were alone together for the first time. One night we got very mellow on some good weed and ended up in my bed. When Sam came back – his father recovered, more or less – we felt we had to tell him. He was furious. He accused us both of betraying him, of destroying the wonderful, unique relationship we'd had between the three of us. Ellie and I tried to tell Sam that we hadn't planned it, that it had just happened, but he wouldn't be mollified. Until . . .

FANNY

Until Ellie offered to sleep with him too.

ADRIAN

Yes. She said that then we'd all be back on equal terms. I'll never forget Sam's face when she said it. We were both lost in wonderment, as a matter of fact. It seemed such a magnanimous gesture. It seemed to abolish the jealousy thing, the possessiveness thing, at a stroke. It was the sixties, you know: we thought we were reinventing sexual relationships. So the next night I made myself scarce, and Ellie went to bed with Sam. He and I never discussed it afterwards, and we went back to being a chaste, platonic threesome. But of course it wasn't the same. We had eaten the apple, or at least taken a large bite out of it. Eventually, Ellie had to choose between us.

69

FANNY

In the novel, the girl goes on sleeping with both of
the men for quite a long time.

ADRIAN

That's all invented. Anyway, after a great deal
of frustration, unhappy experiments with other
relationships, and so on, Ellie chose me. In the
novel, of course, she doesn't marry either of them,
and they all go their different ways.

Pause.

FANNY

That was fascinating. Thank you.

ADRIAN

Now I think you should tell me something equally
. . . personal about yourself.

FANNY

Why?

ADRIAN

It seems only fair.

FANNY

What d'you want to know?

ADRIAN

Well . . . tell me about your tattoo.

FANNY

My butterfly?

ADRIAN

I couldn't help noticing it in the sauna. Did you
have it done for the Essex girl inside you struggling
to get out?

FANNY

No, I did it to please my boyfriend.

ADRIAN

Creighton?

FANNY

God, no, it was years ago. I was between school and university. I went a bit wild, that year. His name was Bruce. He was a rock musician, covered in tattoos. He kept on at me to have one too, and I was so besotted that I agreed. It's a real bore. Means I can't wear sleeveless dresses in the summer.

ADRIAN

Oh, I think it's rather charming. It looks as if the butterfly has just alighted on your shoulder.

FANNY

Unfortunately it's got Bruce's initials stencilled on its wings.

ADRIAN

I didn't notice that.

FANNY

It tends to become a tedious conversational topic at cocktail parties.

ADRIAN

Yes, I can see that could be embarrassing. Is it quite irremovable?

FANNY

Short of a skin graft, yes.

FANNY *slips her bathrobe off her shoulder to squint at the tattoo.*

FANNY

Bruce branded me for life, damn him.

ADRIAN *comes close to* FANNY *to examine the tattoo.*

ADRIAN

'B. B.'

FANNY

Bruce Baxter.

ADRIAN

It's rather exquisitely done, you know. Did it hurt?

FANNY
It was agony.

ADRIAN
And now?

FANNY
Oh, I feel nothing now.

ADRIAN *puts out a finger and traces the outline of the tattoo.*
ELEANOR *appears at the kitchen door, and takes in the scene. She throws her car keys on to the table.* ADRIAN *whirls round, and* FANNY *hastily pulls the robe back to cover her shoulder. They separate.*

ELEANOR
Am I interrupting something?

ADRIAN
Ellie! I didn't hear the car.

ELEANOR
No, it broke down just outside the village. I walked across the fields.

ADRIAN
This is Fanny Tarrant.

ELEANOR
I thought it might be.

ADRIAN
We've just had a sauna.

ELEANOR
How nice.

ADRIAN
What's the matter with the car?

ELEANOR
I don't know. I think it probably just ran out of petrol.

FANNY *conceals a smile.* ADRIAN *catches her eye and grins.*

ELEANOR
Have I said something funny?

ADRIAN
No, it's just . . . never mind.

FANNY
I'd better get dressed. Excuse me.

FANNY *goes out through kitchen.*

ADRIAN
I wasn't expecting you back so soon.

ELEANOR
Evidently.

ADRIAN
Ellie! Don't be silly.

ELEANOR
Rosemary had one of her migraines so I came home early. What does she look like in the nude?

ADRIAN
I really couldn't say. It's quite dark in the sauna, as you know.

ELEANOR
What about in the shower?

ADRIAN
I didn't take a shower with her. I stayed in the sauna after she'd . . . I don't know why I'm playing this silly game. I'm going to get dressed.

ADRIAN *makes to follow* FANNY, *then changes his mind and goes out through the door into the hall and turns towards the stairs.* ELEANOR *notices Fanny's tape-recorder on the coffee table, picks it up, and weighs it in her hand, as if wondering what it contains, then glances at* ADRIAN's *hi-fi system. Its operating light is on.* ELEANOR *goes across to the hi-fi. She presses the Play button on the tape deck. The hiss of a blank tape being played comes from the loudspeakers. She presses the Rewind button. She presses the Stop button and the Play button again.*

ELEANOR'S VOICE
. . . probably just ran out of petrol. (*Pause*) Have I said something funny?

> ADRIAN'S VOICE
> No, it's just . . . never mind.

> FANNY'S VOICE
> I'd better get dressed . . . Excuse me.

ELEANOR *presses the Rewind button again for a few seconds. She presses the Stop button and the Play button.*

> FANNY'S VOICE
> . . . a rock musician, covered in tattoos. He kept on at me to have one too, and I was so besotted that I agreed. It's a real bore. Means I can't wear sleeveless dresses in the summer.

> ADRIAN'S VOICE
> Oh, I think it's rather charming. (ELEANOR *pulls a derisive face*) It looks as if the butterfly has just alighted on your shoulder.

ELEANOR *presses the Stop button, and starts to clear up the juice, glasses, etc. But she decides to have one more go at the tape-recording. She presses the Rewind button for several seconds, then the Stop button, then the Play button.*

> ADRIAN'S VOICE
> . . . seemed to abolish the jealousy thing, the possessiveness thing, at a stroke. It was the sixties, you know: we thought we were reinventing sexual relationships. So the next night I made myself scarce, and Ellie went to bed with Sam. He and I never discussed it afterwards, and—

ELEANOR *presses the Stop button, cutting off the sound. She looks shocked, then angry.* ADRIAN *appears at the door to the hall, dressed in different clothes from earlier in the scene. He is wearing bicycle clips.*

> ADRIAN
> I'll take a can of petrol to the car and see if it starts.

ELEANOR, *her back to* ADRIAN, *does not respond.*

> ADRIAN
> Where is it exactly? This side of the village?

(ELEANOR *still doesn't respond.* ADRIAN *comes into the room*) Ellie?

ELEANOR
How could you?

ADRIAN
What?

ELEANOR
Betray me like that.

ADRIAN
For God's sake, Ellie, it was only a sauna! Nothing happened.

ELEANOR
I'm not talking about the bloody sauna. I mean telling her about *me*, about my private life.

ADRIAN
What d'you mean?

ELEANOR *presses the Play button on hi-fi.*

ADRIAN'S VOICE
. . . and we went back to being a chaste, platonic threesome. But of course it wasn't the same. We had eaten the apple, or at least taken a large bite out of it.

ADRIAN *looks dismayed.*

FANNY'S VOICE
In the novel—

ADRIAN *switches off the hi-fi.*

ADRIAN
That was off the record.

ELEANOR (*points to hi-fi*)
It's *on* the bloody record!

ADRIAN
I mean, she switched off her own tape-recorder for that bit. I forgot mine was still on.

75

ELEANOR

I don't care what was on or off. You told a total
stranger something very private about me, about *me*,
without my permission.

ADRIAN

I'm sorry, Ellie. But—

ELEANOR

It's outrageous. I can hardly believe it.

ADRIAN

Ellie, listen. I let something slip out about our
student days, Sam and I meeting you, and she was
on to it in a flash—

ELEANOR

Surprise, surprise.

ADRIAN

I thought it was best to set her straight, off the
record. That way, she can't use any of it.

ELEANOR

Why would she be interested in anything she
can't use?

ADRIAN

I asked her that. It turns out she's a bit of a fan,
actually . . .

ELEANOR

Oh, how nice! Did she bring you a book to sign?

ADRIAN

Well, as it happens, she did.

ELEANOR

For God's sake! You're as bad as Sam! What else
did you tell her? Did you tell her I had an abortion?

ADRIAN (*shocked*)

Of course I didn't. (*He glances towards the kitchen
door*)

ELEANOR

What stopped you?

ADRIAN (*lowers his voice*)
We don't speak of that even between ourselves.

ELEANOR
Supposing she finds out on her own?

ADRIAN
She won't. She can't. In any case the whole story of
you and me and Sam is ring-fenced. She gave me
her word.

ELEANOR
And you trust her?

ADRIAN
Yes.

FANNY *comes through the kitchen door, dressed.* ELEANOR *turns
aside and struggles to compose herself.*

ADRIAN
Oh, there you are. (*He moves towards the door to hall*)
I'm just going to put some petrol in the car. If it
starts I can run you to the station.

FANNY
Thanks, but you needn't bother.

ADRIAN (*goes out*)
No bother. Back in two ticks.

FANNY
No, please, I—

Sound of front door shutting.

FANNY (*to* ELEANOR)
Actually I took the liberty of ringing for a cab from
the kitchen.

ELEANOR
What train are you catching?

FANNY
The first that comes.

ELEANOR (*glances at her watch*)
You've just missed one. You'll have to wait for

nearly an hour. Unless you take the taxi all the way to Gatwick.

FANNY
Then I'll do that.

Pause.

FANNY
This is rather awkward.

ELEANOR
Yes.

FANNY
I hope you didn't jump to any conclusions . . .

ELEANOR
What sort of conclusions?

FANNY
We had a sauna, that's all. There was nothing . . . sexual about it.

ELEANOR
You don't see anything sexual about sitting stark naked in a small wooden box with a strange man?

FANNY
I felt quite comfortable. There was no touching or anything.

ELEANOR
He seemed to be touching you when I came in.

FANNY
I was showing him a tattoo I have on my shoulder.

ELEANOR
I see. Well, it makes a change from etchings, I suppose.

FANNY
Look, I'm sorry. In retrospect it was probably not a good idea, the sauna, but he sort of dared me, and I never could resist a dare.

ELEANOR

Why did you come here?

FANNY *goes across to coffee table and picks up her tape-recorder.*

FANNY

To interview your husband.

ELEANOR

Yes, but why him? He's not a well-known author
any more.

FANNY

That was what interested me. I wanted to find out
why he stopped writing.

ELEANOR

And did you?

FANNY

I think so. He told me he didn't have anything left
to say that seemed worth the bother of thinking up
another story to say it with.

FANNY *picks up her briefcase and opens it preparatory to putting
her tape-recorder in it.*

ELEANOR

Did he, indeed?

FANNY

Not many writers have such humility.

ELEANOR (*scornfully, sceptically*)

Huh!

FANNY

You don't agree?

FANNY's *interest is alerted, but she disguises it with a casual tone.*
ELEANOR *is still fizzing with anger.*

ELEANOR

I've spent too many hours trying to prop up his
self-esteem.

Unobserved by ELEANOR, FANNY *switches on her tape-recorder.*

FANNY

Well, Virginia Woolf says somewhere that the worst
thing about being a writer is that one is so dependent
on praise.

ELEANOR

It's the worst thing about being married to one, too.
If you don't enthuse about their work they sulk, and
if you do they don't think it really counts.

FANNY (*smiles*)

Which it doesn't, of course. Not like reviews.

ELEANOR

Adrian got wonderful reviews for his first book. It
was the worst thing that could have happened to
him. He kept thinking it would happen again, that
royal flush of rave reviews. It didn't. Each novel was
a worse ordeal than the one before. The tension in
the house was unbearable around publication day.
He used to sit on the stairs in the early morning in
his pyjamas and dressing-gown, waiting for the paper
to come through the letter-box. Then as soon as I
was up, he'd send me out to get the other papers.

FANNY

Why didn't he get them himself?

ELEANOR

Because he liked to pretend to other people that he
didn't bother reading reviews, that he left all that
to me. And, for a while, I did take on the job. But
it was no use, he would get them out of the filing
cabinet when I wasn't around, and I could tell from
his gloom as he mooched about the house that he'd
discovered a bad one.

FANNY

He must have been difficult to live with.

ELEANOR

Difficult! He was bloody impossible. No wonder
the boys left home as soon as they could . . .

Between the agony of composition and the ordeal of publication there was a period of about three months when he was like a normal human being. Then the whole cycle would start again.

FANNY

Why did it stop with *Out of the Depths*?

ELEANOR

His publishers were very pleased with it, and some idiot there put it into Adrian's head that he was going to win the Booker Prize, and God knows what else. Well, when it came out, it got the usual mixed reception – some good reviews, some not so good, a few nasty ones from young smartypants out to make names for themselves – and it wasn't even shortlisted for the Booker. Adrian went into a deep depression – which I had to try and conceal from his publisher, his agent, his friends, and the rest of the world. I just couldn't take it any more.

FANNY

You threatened to leave him?

ELEANOR

It amounted to that. But he'd decided he couldn't take it any more either. He said he was finished with writing fiction. We sold our London house and moved down here, to start a different kind of life . . . So. It was a solution, but not exactly a heroic one.

FANNY

I'm disappointed, I admit.

ELEANOR

Why?

FANNY

Well, he was a kind of hero to me once.

ELEANOR *looks uneasy: she is beginning to regret her outburst. Sound of doorchime off.*

FANNY

That's probably my taxi.

Act Two Scene One

FANNY *switches off her tape-recorder.* ELEANOR *notices this, and panics.*

> ELEANOR
>
> You haven't been taping me, have you?

> FANNY
>
> Yes.

> ELEANOR
>
> You didn't ask my permission.

> FANNY
>
> What difference does it make?

> ELEANOR
>
> You had no right.

> FANNY
>
> You didn't say it was off the record.

> ELEANOR
>
> I know, but . . .

> FANNY
>
> But what? Why did you tell me all that stuff?

> ELEANOR
>
> I was upset.

> FANNY
>
> You were pissed off with your husband so you shopped him to me.

FANNY *puts the tape-recorder in her briefcase and closes it.*

> ELEANOR
>
> Give me the tape. Or erase the bit with me on it.

> FANNY (*shakes head*)
>
> Sorry.

Doorchime sounds again.

> FANNY
>
> I must go.

ELEANOR

Look, I suppose I wanted you to know the truth. But I didn't necessarily mean you to publish it.

FANNY (*sardonically*)

'Necessarily'?

ELEANOR

Please.

FANNY

You know what I do for a living.

Pause. The two women hold each other's gaze.

ELEANOR

Yes, you destroy people's lives. You flatter them rotten and insinuate yourself into their homes, and lure them into making unguarded remarks and betray their confidence and wreck their self-esteem and ruin their peace of mind. That's what you do for a living.

Doorchime sounds again.

FANNY

Goodbye.

FANNY *goes out through hall. Sound of front door slamming.*
ELEANOR *stands frozen, appalled at what she has done.*

Blackout.

Act Two Scene Two. Thirteen days later, early morning.

The living-room of the cottage. In the distance a cock crows.
ELEANOR *is sitting at the table in her dressing-gown, with a mug half-full of cold coffee in front of her. She looks anxious and tense. She hears the sound of a car approaching, slowly and quietly. It stops.* ELEANOR *darts into the hall and turns out of sight towards the front door. Sound of car door being shut with minimum noise.*

Act Two Scene Two

Sound of the bolts on the front door being drawn, and the door opened.

> ELEANOR (*off*)
> Good God, you of all people.

> SAM (*off*)
> It's terribly early, I know, but—

> ELEANOR (*off*)
> Come in.

Sound of front door being closed. SAM *comes into the room, talking. He is unshaven, his clothes crumpled. He is not wearing his toupee.*

> SAM
> I just flew in from LA on the red-eye. Thought I'd collect my pot, if you were up and about. Which you are.

> ELEANOR (*following him in*)
> You said you were going for a month.

> SAM
> My plans changed. How are you, anyway?

SAM *leans forward to kiss* ELEANOR *on the cheek. She pulls away.*

> ELEANOR
> I don't want to kiss you, Sam.

> SAM
> Oh. Stubble? Bad breath?

> ELEANOR
> I'm angry with you.

> SAM
> Why? What have I done?

> ELEANOR
> You introduced that poisonous snake Fanny Tarrant into our lives.

> SAM (*surprised*)
> You mean – she took the bait?

ELEANOR

Yes.

SAM (*eagerly*)

And did Adrian write his article about her?

ELEANOR

Not as far as I know. But Fanny Tarrant wrote hers about him.

SAM

Show me.

ELEANOR

I haven't got it. That's why I'm up at this ungodly hour. I'm waiting for the Sunday papers to be delivered.

SAM

How d'you know it'll be in today's paper?

ELEANOR

It was trailed in last Sunday's: 'Fanny Tarrant tracks Adrian Ludlow to his Hideaway'.

SAM

That sounds all right. It might be quite a nice piece.

ELEANOR

It won't be.

SAM

How do you know?

ELEANOR

It's a long story. I'll try and make it short.

SAM

Can I have some coffee?

ELEANOR

No.

SAM

No?

ELEANOR
Listen, damn you!

SAM (*submissively*)
All right. (*He sits down*)

ELEANOR
Your stupid plot worked, up to a point. Adrian's agent fixed up the interview — (ELEANOR *stares at* SAM) Where's your toupee?

SAM
I binned it.

ELEANOR (*continuing her story*)
Fanny Tarrant came down here. I arranged to be out for the day. But I came home earlier than expected.

Pause, as ELEANOR *recalls the moment.*

SAM
Don't tell me you found them in bed together.

ELEANOR
Not quite such a cliché as that. But they had just had a sauna together.

SAM
A sauna? You mean, in the nude?

ELEANOR
So I understand.

SAM (*tone of envy and admiration*)
Bloody hell!

ELEANOR
They were lolling about in bathrobes when I walked in. Hers was fetchingly off the shoulder because she was showing him her tattoo.

SAM
What kind of tattoo?

ELEANOR (*irritably*)
What does it matter?

SAM
Just curious.

ELEANOR
A butterfly.

SAM
Moves like a butterfly, stings like a bee.

ELEANOR
More like a scorpion. She ought to have a scorpion
tail tattooed on her behind . . . While they were
getting dressed, I played back a bit of Adrian's tape-
recording of the interview, and I couldn't believe it
– he was talking about us – I mean about when we
were students. When, you know . . .

SAM
What?

ELEANOR
When I slept with Adrian and then with you.

SAM
Jesus! Is he crazy?

ELEANOR
He says it was off the record.

SAM (*relieved*)
Oh, off the record. (*Beat*) You don't trust her?

ELEANOR
No. I don't know. The point is, he had no right to
tell her *anything* about me, let alone something as
private as that.

SAM
No of course not, but—

ELEANOR
For years I put up with coming across bits of my
private life in his novels. But at least I could tell
myself that nobody else would know, because he'd

changed things and jumbled them up. But *this* was
something else . . .

SAM

I understand why you're mad. But really, there's no
need to get in a state about the paper.

ELEANOR

You don't know what's in it.

SAM

Even if she's used the story, it's not going to make
any waves. So you slept with two boyfriends, one
after the other, thirty years ago. So what? Who cares?
(ELEANOR *is silent*) He didn't tell her anything else,
did he?

ELEANOR

No.

SAM

Thank Christ for that. So what are you worried
about?

ELEANOR

I haven't finished telling you.

SAM

Oh. Go on.

ELEANOR

Well, while she was waiting for her taxi and Adrian
was fetching the car—

SAM

Where was the car, then?

ELEANOR

What does it matter where the bloody car was?

SAM

Sorry. If you're a scriptwriter you get in the habit of
asking these questions.

ELEANOR

I ran out of petrol just outside the village. I walked

home across the fields. (*She points in the appropriate direction*) Adrian took a can of petrol to the car. Satisfied?

SAM

So you surprised them in their bathrobes because they didn't hear the car coming. You see: it all fits together.

ELEANOR

This isn't one of your scripts, Sam, it's my life.

SAM

Mine too, by the sound of it. So what happened while—

ELEANOR (*holds up her hand*)

Ssh!

SAM

What?

ELEANOR *goes towards window and looks out.*

ELEANOR

Nothing. (*She returns to previous position*) I thought I heard Mr Barnes's van.

SAM

Who's Mr Barnes?

ELEANOR

Our newsagent.

SAM

Oh. So what happened while Adrian was getting the car?

ELEANOR

I was left with the Tarrant woman. I was angry, upset. She said Adrian told her that he gave up writing novels because he'd decided he had nothing new to say. She seemed so pleased with herself at having made this discovery, and so admiring of Adrian, it made me sick. So I blurted out the *real* reason why he stopped writing.

Beat.

> SAM
>
> Why did he?

> ELEANOR
>
> Don't you know? Haven't you guessed?

> SAM
>
> Some kind of block, I presume.

> ELEANOR
>
> No. He just couldn't stand being continually
> reminded that nothing he wrote was as good as his
> first book.

> SAM
>
> You mean reviews? Adrian always said he never read
> reviews.

> ELEANOR
>
> A complete lie. Which I connived at. But it wasn't
> just reviews. Any kind of slight, real or imagined,
> would send him into despair. When *Out of the Depths*
> wasn't shortlisted for the Booker he was practically
> suicidal.

> SAM
>
> I had no idea . . . And you told Fanny Tarrant
> all this?

> ELEANOR
>
> Yes.

> SAM
>
> Off the record?

> ELEANOR
>
> No.

> SAM
>
> Oh dear.

> ELEANOR
>
> I was angry. I wasn't thinking clearly. I didn't realise

she was taping me until she switched her machine
off. When Adrian came back, after she'd gone, I
confessed what I'd done.

SAM
What did he say?

ELEANOR
He didn't say anything. He hasn't spoken to
me since.

SAM
About Fanny Tarrant?

ELEANOR
About anything. He hasn't addressed a single word
to me on any subject whatsoever since that day,
except when other people are present. Then he chats
away, and smiles and laughs and draws me into the
conversation as if everything were perfectly normal,
but as soon as the other people have gone, whether
it's neighbours or the vicar or our cleaning lady, he
goes stony silent, ignores what I say, and leaves me
little notes.

ELEANOR *digs into the pocket of her dressing-gown and pulls out a
handful of folded and crumpled pieces of paper. She lets them fall
from her hand.* SAM *picks one up and opens it.*

SAM (*reads*)
'I shall require the car tomorrow morning between
11.30 a.m. and 1 p.m.' Why d'you put up with this
nonsense? Why don't you push off and leave him to
stew in his own juice?

ELEANOR
Because I feel guilty, I suppose. For betraying
his secret.

SAM
You didn't mean to.

ELEANOR
I did really. I just changed my mind, too late.

SAM
Well, he provoked you . . . Where is he now?

ELEANOR
Still asleep, I expect. He sleeps in the guest room,
goes to bed hours after me and gets up late, so we
don't have breakfast at the same time. We don't have
any meals together, actually.

SAM
Ellie, come home with me. Now. Leave *him* a note.
That'll bring him to his senses.

ELEANOR
No thanks, Sam.

SAM
You're letting him treat you as some kind of
criminal. It's absurd.

ELEANOR
I know, but . . .

SAM
Get dressed, pack a bag, come with me now. While
he's still asleep. Just do it. (ELEANOR *shakes her
head*) No strings attached. Unless you want them, of
course.

ELEANOR (*smiles*)
Thanks, Sam, but I can't.

SAM
Why not?

ELEANOR
If I left now, I'd never come back. That would be
the end.

SAM
Well, maybe you've come to the end of this
marriage.

ELEANOR
Oh, I don't want a divorce, Sam! Everybody I know
has been divorced. I've seen what it does to people.

You know what it's like. I don't want to go through
all that, not at my time of life. I should have done it
ten or fifteen years ago, if I was going to do it.

SAM

But if the marriage has gone sour—

ELEANOR

No, since we came to live here, it's improved a lot.
Adrian can be lovely when he's in a good mood.

SAM

Oh, I know that.

ELEANOR

And since he gave up writing novels he's been in a
good mood nearly all the time, or he's pretended to
be, which amounts to the same thing as far as I'm
concerned.

SAM

Why did you marry him, Ellie?

ELEANOR

He was the father.

SAM

What?

ELEANOR

When I had the abortion.

SAM

You said you didn't know which of us was
the father.

ELEANOR

But I did know. I was protected when I slept
with you.

SAM

But not when you slept with Adrian? (ELEANOR *nods*)
Jesus, why didn't you say at the time?

ELEANOR

I thought it was the best thing to do. I thought

93

you would both support me, that it would keep us
together as a trio, if neither of you knew who was
the father. You know, like the blank cartridge in
the firing squad. Or the opposite. (SAM *is stunned*) I
was a very muddled, panic-stricken young woman.
I just wanted to be un-pregnant. But later I got very
depressed about it. One day I told Adrian that he
had been the father, and he asked me to marry him.

SAM

So that you could have children?

ELEANOR

Yes. I sometimes wonder if the first pregnancy was a
girl. I would have liked a girl.

SAM

She might have turned out like Fanny Tarrant.

ELEANOR

Don't joke about it, Sam.

SAM

How should I react, then?

ELEANOR

What d'you mean?

SAM

I could be angry, if you like.

ELEANOR

Oh.

SAM

Jesus, Ellie! You deceived me.

ELEANOR

I know. I'm sorry.

SAM

And you let me stay deceived.

ELEANOR

I was trying to deceive myself, pretend it never
happened.

94

SAM

I've made enough real mistakes in my life. I could
have done without my fifty per cent share in
that one.

ELEANOR

I'm sorry, Sam.

SAM

OK.

ELEANOR

You're not angry, are you?

SAM

No, I'm not angry.

Pause.

SAM

How much longer are you going to put up with
Adrian freezing you out?

ELEANOR

Not much longer. However ghastly Fanny Tarrant's
article is, it won't be as bad as waiting for it to
appear. I have a feeling that, once we know the
worst, the spell will be lifted. Adrian will speak to me
again, and we'll sort it out.

SAM

And if you don't?

ELEANOR

Then I might be glad of your guest room.

Pause.

SAM

When do your papers usually come?

ELEANOR

You can never tell. It all depends on whether Mr
Barnes delivers them himself in his van, or sends his
boy on a bicycle.

95

SAM

Why don't I drive into the village and get the
Sentinel now?

ELEANOR

The shop won't be open yet.

SAM

There'll be one open somewhere.

ELEANOR

Not at this hour, on a Sunday. Not for miles.

SAM

Do you want me to stay till the paper comes? Or
would you prefer to be alone?

Beat.

ELEANOR

Stay.

SAM

Can I have some coffee, then?

ELEANOR (*smiles*)

Yes, of course. I'll make a fresh pot.

ELEANOR *moves towards the kitchen.*

SAM

I need to wash up, as the Yanks say.

ELEANOR

Use the loo at the back. Through here. (ELEANOR
leads SAM *into the kitchen*)

SAM

Right.

They go out. After a brief interval ADRIAN, *in dressing-gown and
pyjamas, having come downstairs, passes the open door leading
to the hall, walking towards the front door. Almost immediately,
he comes back and enters the living-room. He looks around as if
in search of something.* ELEANOR *comes in from the kitchen with a
tray bearing crockery and cutlery. She stops and looks at* ADRIAN.

ELEANOR
If you're looking for the papers, they haven't
come yet.

ADRIAN *ignores her. He takes an old magazine out of the magazine
rack and sits down in an armchair. He pretends to read the
magazine.* ELEANOR *unloads her tray at the table.*

ELEANOR
I'm making some coffee and toast. Do you
want some?

ADRIAN *continues to ignore her.*

ELEANOR
Sam's here.

ADRIAN *reacts sharply and stares at* ELEANOR.

ELEANOR
He's in the loo.

ADRIAN *turns back to his magazine.*

ELEANOR
I've told him everything, so you might as well give
up this silly game.

ADRIAN *continues to ignore* ELEANOR. *She bangs down the last
item from her tray and goes back into the kitchen.* ADRIAN *stops
pretending to read. He is obviously discomposed. After a brief
interval,* SAM *comes in from the kitchen.*

SAM
Adrian! You're up.

ADRIAN (*coldly*)
What are you doing here?

SAM
I flew in from LA this morning. Dropped in on the
off-chance, to collect my pot.

ADRIAN
I thought you were supposed to be away for a
month.

SAM
Change of plan.

ADRIAN
You mean the studio fired you?

SAM
No, I fired them. In a manner of speaking.

ADRIAN
What manner of speaking?

SAM (*puts down vase*)
I checked out. I decided I didn't want to become
a Hollywood whore. There I was, sitting under a
parasol beside my private pool in Beverly Hills,
working on the umpteenth draft of a lesbian
love scene between Florence Nightingale and a
young nurse—

ADRIAN
Was Florence Nightingale a lesbian?

SAM
She is in this movie. Anyway, there I was pegging
away on my laptop, when I suddenly thought to
myself: what am I doing wasting my time on this
crap? I mean, sure I'll make a lot of money out of it,
but who knows if it will ever be made and whether
they'll use my lines if it *is* made and who will care
anyway in ten years' time?

ADRIAN
A kind of road-to-Damascus experience.

SAM
That's right. I feel born again.

ADRIAN
You mean, bald again.

SAM
Hah hah! I realised that I was in danger of becoming
a scriptwriting machine.

ADRIAN (*struck by an echo*)

You mean, by turning out scripts like cars off a production line, you don't give yourself time to take stock of the *quality* of what you're producing?

SAM

Yeah, exactly.

ADRIAN

Well, well. And what are you going to do about it?

SAM

Take a sabbatical for a year or two. Say no to all new script offers. Do some serious reading and thinking. Maybe write a novel.

ADRIAN

A novel?

SAM

Yeah, I've always wanted to try my hand at a novel.

ADRIAN

So you won't be offering to adapt *The Hideaway* for the BBC?

SAM

Er, no, not for the time being. (*This reminds* SAM *of why he made the offer*) Sorry about that. I gather our plot against Fanny Tarrant rather misfired.

ADRIAN

Yes.

SAM

Did Peter Reeves at the *Chronicle* get in touch?

ADRIAN

Yes.

SAM

Wasn't he interested?

ADRIAN

Oh yes. But the worst I could discover about Fanny

Tarrant was that she went to a convent boarding-school, not a comprehensive; that she lives with a man called Creighton; and that she has a butterfly tattooed on her shoulder with the initials of a former rock star on its wings. Not much ammunition for a devastating exposé there, you must admit.

SAM

But you gave *her* some, I hear.

ADRIAN

Eleanor did.

SAM

Oh, come on, Adrian, be fair. *You* told Fanny Tarrant about the three of us at university.

ADRIAN

That was off the record.

SAM

But why tell her anyway?

ADRIAN

Damage limitation. She was on the scent . . .

SAM

And why the sauna?

ADRIAN

I thought if I sprang something totally unexpected on her, she might reveal something unexpected about herself.

SAM

You really took that reverse-interview idea seriously, didn't you?

ADRIAN

You sound surprised.

SAM

Well, frankly, I'm amazed that you went through with it. And very upset that it all went wrong.

ADRIAN

You're upset?

SAM

Well, I instigated the whole thing. I feel responsible.

ADRIAN

Perhaps you'd like to sort it out, then. Arrange to
buy up every edition of today's *Sunday Sentinel*
and have them incinerated. Go round the country
from door to door buying back the copies already
delivered at an irresistible premium. Administer
amnesia-inducing drugs to those householders who
have already read Fanny Tarrant's article. (*Looks
at watch*) I should get started, if I were you. You
haven't got a lot of time.

SAM

All right, I can't undo the damage that's already
been done. But perhaps I can help you come to
terms with it.

ADRIAN

I very much doubt it.

SAM

You can prepare yourself psychologically. Fear is
your worst enemy.

ADRIAN

Did you by any chance go into therapy while you
were in California?

SAM

What's the worst thing she can say about you? That
you gave up writing because you couldn't bear
criticism.

ADRIAN

Is this supposed to be making me feel better?

SAM

That's the worst she can say. Can you look it in the
eye and accept it?

Pause.

ADRIAN

No, since you ask. No, I can't accept it. I can't bear
the thought of half a million people knowing that
about me. I can't help my weakness, I'm ashamed
of it, but I did manage to keep it to myself for
twenty years.

ELEANOR *comes in with coffee and toast.*

ADRIAN

Ah, coffee and toast! I expect you've already had a
champagne breakfast somewhere over the Irish Sea,
Sam, but perhaps you'll partake of our humble fare.
Shall we sit up at the table, Ellie?

ELEANOR (*with controlled anger*)

Adrian, if you go on in that plummy mine host
manner a minute longer, I swear to God I'll throw
this coffee pot at you.

ADRIAN

I don't know what you mean, my dear.

ELEANOR

Sam, leave the room.

SAM

What?

ELEANOR

Just do as I say! Go into the hall and wait there.

SAM

Wait for—?

ELEANOR

Go!

SAM *goes meekly out of the room into the hall, closing the
door behind him.*

ELEANOR

Either you start speaking to me like a normal human
being, or I'm going to leave now, instantly, this
minute. (*Beat*) Sam has invited me to stay with him.

ADRIAN *is silent. After a pause,* ELEANOR *moves towards the door.*

> ADRIAN
>
> All right.

> ELEANOR *(stops and turns)*
>
> Did you speak?

> ADRIAN
>
> I said 'all right'.

> ELEANOR
>
> All right what?

> ADRIAN
>
> All right, I'll speak to you like a normal human being. I've spoken.

Pause. ELEANOR *moves back into the room.*

> ELEANOR
>
> Do you know, I was actually hoping that you wouldn't. So I could walk out of here with a clear conscience.

> ADRIAN
>
> I'm sorry.

> ELEANOR
>
> You've been a real swine these last two weeks.

> ADRIAN
>
> I know.

> ELEANOR
>
> It's not as if I *wanted* to come and live down here. I didn't *want* to give up my job at the V & A, I didn't *want* to lose touch with my friends, and give up going to the theatre and galleries and shopping whenever I felt like it. I did it for *your* sake. To give you peace. To keep you sane. And what thanks do I get? You blow it all away, just to gratify your vanity. And when I react you have the nerve to, to . . .

SAM *comes back into the room in the course of this speech.* ELEANOR

sinks on to the nearest chair and sobs. ADRIAN *moves towards her,
but as* ELEANOR's *sobs become louder* SAM *gets to her first.*

> SAM (*pushing* ADRIAN out of the way)
> Ellie, what's the matter?

> ADRIAN
> Hey, mind!

> SAM (*accusingly to* ADRIAN)
> What did you do to her?

> ADRIAN
> Nothing.

> SAM
> Why is she sobbing her heart out?

SAM *embraces* ELEANOR *protectively.* ADRIAN *pulls her away
from him.*

> ADRIAN
> It's none of your business.

> SAM
> You know, sometimes I find it hard to believe we
> were ever friends.

> ADRIAN
> Strangely enough, I have the same problem.

They stop tugging at ELEANOR *and stand to confront each other.*

> SAM
> You've become a pompous, selfish, supercilious prat.

> ADRIAN
> And you've turned into a vain, swaggering,
> unprincipled twerp. Fanny Tarrant had you cold.

ELEANOR *begins to compose herself. She takes a tissue from her
dressing-gown pocket and blows her nose.*

> SAM
> Well, I'm really looking forward to seeing what
> she has to say about *you*. (*Beat*) What d'you mean,
> unprincipled?

ADRIAN

You sold your soul to television for the sake of popular success.

SAM

I'd rather be a popular success than a high-minded failure. You're afraid I'll write a popular, successful novel now, aren't you?

ADRIAN

The idea of your writing a novel is so—

ELEANOR (*loudly*)

Shut up, both of you! (*She holds up her hand in a silencing gesture*)

They freeze. Sound of a motor vehicle approaching and drawing up outside the cottage. ELEANOR *hurries into the hall and turns towards the front door.* ADRIAN *looks anxiously after her, then sits down.* SAM *and* ADRIAN *sit staring into space.*

Pause.

SAM

What does she look like in the nude?

ADRIAN

Oh, for God's sake.

SAM

No, I'm interested.

ADRIAN

I didn't particularly notice.

SAM

Oh, come off it, Adrian! Are you telling me you persuaded Fanny Tarrant to take her kit off and you didn't notice the size of her boobs, or the shape of her bum? Does she shave her pubic hair?

FANNY, *casually dressed, appears at the door to the hall, and stands on the threshold, listening to* SAM's *speech.*

SAM (*grins lasciviously*)

I bet she does. I bet Fanny Tarrant shaves her

bikini-line religiously every Friday night, leaving just
a narrow tuft of hair on her pubes, like a vertical
moustache. Am I right?

FANNY

Wrong.

SAM *and* ADRIAN, *startled, whirl round, jump to their feet and gape
at* FANNY.

SAM

What the fuck are you doing here?

FANNY *enters the room, followed by* ELEANOR, *who looks hard at*
ADRIAN. FANNY *looks pale and has a slightly wild, distracted air.*

FANNY

I happened to be in the neighbourhood. But I wasn't
expecting to meet you, Mr Sharp.

ELEANOR (*to* ADRIAN)

Did you invite her here?

ADRIAN

Of course not.

SAM

Perhaps she left something in the sauna.

FANNY (*to* ADRIAN)

I presume you've read it – my piece about you?

ADRIAN

No. Our papers haven't come yet.

FANNY (*disconcerted*)

Oh. Well, I shouldn't bother, if I were you. It's not
very nice. The thing is, nobody will take any notice
of it. (*She looks longingly at the table*) Is that coffee,
by any chance?

ELEANOR

What's this all about? You're not welcome here.

SAM

To put it mildly.

FANNY
I'm dying for a cup of coffee.

ELEANOR
Take some, then. But don't expect me to pour it
for you.

FANNY *moves eagerly to the table and pours herself a cup of coffee.*

ELEANOR
What have you written about Adrian?

FANNY
Can't you guess? My teenage idol who turned out
to have feet of clay. The man who would make his
family's life a misery because of a bad review. The
writer who had to get out of the kitchen because
he couldn't stand the heat, but pretended he'd lost
interest in cooking. (ADRIAN *stiffens as he listens to this.*)

SAM
A Fanny Tarrant Special, in other words.

FANNY (*drinking the coffee*)
God, I needed that.

ELEANOR
Is that all?

FANNY (*surprised*)
Isn't it enough?

ELEANOR
There's . . . nothing about us when we were
students?

FANNY
That was off the record. Could I possibly have
some toast?

ELEANOR (*shrugs bemusedly*)
Help yourself.

SAM
Can we get you anything else? How about some
eggs? D'you like them sunny side up or easy over?

FANNY (*tucking into toast*)

No, this is fine. I think my blood sugar level must be low. I was feeling faint in the car.

SAM

Look, speaking for myself I'm getting tired of this game. Say what you want to say and then fuck off. Or just fuck off.

FANNY *looks at each of them in turn. She looks at the TV set.*

FANNY

You haven't heard yet, have you?

ELEANOR

Heard what?

FANNY

It's strange, it's as if I'm looking at you through a glass wall. You're in a different time zone. You don't know.

ADRIAN

We don't know what?

FANNY

Diana's dead.

ADRIAN

Diana who?

FANNY

Diana, Princess of Wales.

ELEANOR

What?

SAM (*sceptically*)

How?

FANNY

A car crash, in Paris. She was in a car with Dodi, being chased by *paparazzi*. The car skidded in a tunnel, smashed into a concrete column. Dodi was killed too. And their driver.

SAM (*still sceptical*)
When did this happen?

FANNY
Early this morning. I heard it on the car radio, an
hour ago.

ADRIAN
You're quite sure? It's been confirmed?

FANNY
Oh yes. We were on the M23, between Redhill and
Gatwick, going to catch a charter flight to Turkey.
Creighton was driving—

ADRIAN
Creighton? Where's Creighton, then?

FANNY
He's in the car outside, sulking.

ADRIAN
Why is he sulking?

FANNY
Because we're not going to Turkey. I said he could
go on his own, but he didn't want to.

ADRIAN
You cancelled your holiday because of . . . ?

FANNY
I wouldn't dream of leaving the country *now*.

ADRIAN
But why are you here?

FANNY
Creighton was driving. The CD we were listening
to came to an end, and I switched on the radio.
A news anchorman was talking to somebody on a
telephone link about a car crash. It was a minute or
two before we realised who they were talking about,
who was dead. I was totally stunned at first. Then
I thought, 'Nobody will ever be able to criticise her

again.' I said something like that to Creighton, and
he said, 'Yes, good career move,' and I snapped at
him, 'That isn't funny,' much to his surprise. Then
on the radio they went over to Kensington Palace.
There are already people there, laying flowers outside
the gates. The reporter spoke to some of them, asked
them why they'd come. One of them said, 'She
visited the hospital where my little boy was. He had
leukaemia. She held his hand and talked to him.
She was a lovely lady.' I burst into tears. (*She sheds
a few more*) I'm sorry. I don't usually do this. I *hate*
doing it. Creighton thinks I've completely lost my
marbles. He said, 'All right, it's sad, but not *that*
sad.' Then, when I went on crying, he said, 'Is it
your time of the month?' We had this huge row in
a lay-by outside Gatwick. Eventually he turned the
car round and we set off back to London, listening
to the radio in a grim silence. I began to brood about
today's *Sentinel*. There are two things by me in it.
(*To* ADRIAN) The interview with you. And a Diary
piece. The Diary piece is about Diana.

Pause.

SAM

Oh boy.

FANNY

Something about her wanting to have it both ways.
To be the Madonna of the Minefields, nursing
limbless toddlers on her knee, *and* the Playgirl of the
Western World, lolling about in Dodi's speedboat in
a leopard-skin swimsuit . . .

SAM

Lovely. I recognise the style.

FANNY

I'm not the first journalist to have said it, but it's
not something you'd particularly want to see under
your by-line this morning. And anyway, I thought to
myself, why the fuck shouldn't she have had it both

ways? Wouldn't we all like to if we could manage it?
I thought, what a bloody mean-spirited thing to say.
Only it was too late to withdraw it, or apologise for
it. And then I thought about my piece about you . . .
and that seemed pretty mean-spirited too . . . I saw a
road sign to your village. I told Creighton to take the
road. So here I am.

ELEANOR
So what do you want? Our forgiveness?

FANNY
I suppose.

ADRIAN
Well, I don't feel like giving it.

FANNY
I don't blame you.

SAM
Neither do I.

FANNY
I hadn't thought about you, Mr Sharp. I'm not sure
I feel any remorse about *that* piece.

SAM
Well, that's just as well, because I was going to tell
you to stick your remorse up your arse. I never heard
such a lot of sentimental crap in my life.

Sound of car horn, off.

FANNY
I'd better go. (*To* ADRIAN) Look, you needn't feel too
bad about my article, because nobody will read it.

ADRIAN
What d'you mean?

FANNY
Nobody's going to be reading the Sunday papers
today, or if they have already, they won't remember
what's in them. They'll be waiting for tomorrow's

papers, with their tongues hanging out. There's only
one story anybody's interested in right now, and it
isn't yours – or mine. 'Bye.

FANNY *goes out. Sound of front door closing, car engine starting.*
ADRIAN *goes to the window and looks out.* ELEANOR *breaks
the silence.*

> ELEANOR
> I can't believe it.

> SAM
> Fanny Tarrant's conversion on the road to Gatwick?

> ELEANOR
> Diana dead.

> SAM
> Oh.

The sound of the car drawing away.

> ADRIAN (*turns away from window*)
> It's so incredibly poetic. Like a Greek tragedy. You
> don't expect life to imitate art so closely.

> ELEANOR
> Poetic? Being smashed to bits in a car crash?

> ADRIAN
> But pursued by *paparazzi* . . . the Furies of the
> media. And killed with her new lover. Love
> and death.

> ELEANOR
> Must you turn everything into literature? She was a
> real woman, for God's sake, in the prime of life. And
> the mother of two boys.

> ADRIAN
> I didn't think you had much time for her.

> ELEANOR
> Well, I didn't . . . or I thought I didn't. But when
> she told us (*gestures in the direction of the departed*

FANNY) she'd been killed, when she said 'Diana is dead', I felt a pang, as if it was someone I knew personally. It's strange.

SAM

She was a star. It's as simple as that.

ELEANOR

Nothing is as simple as that, Sam.

ELEANOR *switches on the TV (which has its back to the audience) and steps back, holding the remote control, waiting for it to warm up. She sits down on the* chaise-longue *next to* SAM.

ADRIAN (*to* ELEANOR)

Because I read the event like a drama doesn't mean I'm not affected by it. (*Reflectively*) In fact, I'm more affected than I would have thought possible. Not as much as Fanny Tarrant, but still—

SAM

Fanny Tarrant! You didn't buy that penitential act, did you?

ADRIAN

She didn't have to come here. It took some courage.

SAM

Huh! It won't be long before she's back in the denigration business, along with the rest of her tribe.

As the sound of the TV news coverage becomes audible, ADRIAN *sits down on the* chaise-longue *to watch with the other two.*

ADRIAN

I don't know . . . It can make a difference. Even the death of someone you never knew, if it's sufficiently . . .

SAM

Poetic.

ADRIAN

Yes, actually. 'Arousing pity and fear, whereby to provide an outlet for such emotions.'

        SAM (*recognises the quotation*)
  Good old Aristotle!

Pause (while they watch the TV).

        ADRIAN
  We pity the victim and fear for ourselves. It can have
  a powerful effect.

Pause (while they watch the TV).

        SAM
  You think we're in for a national catharsis, then?

        ADRIAN
  Conceivably.

        SAM
  Well, we shall see . . . I think I'll be going, Ellie.
  Where's my pot? (*He gets to his feet*)

        ELEANOR
  Oh, don't go, Sam! Stay.

        SAM (*glances at* ADRIAN)
  Well, I don't know . . .

        ELEANOR
  Adrian.

        ADRIAN (*looking at the TV*)
  What?

        ELEANOR
  Tell Sam to stay.

        ADRIAN (*looking at the TV*)
  Stay.

        SAM
  I'm jet-lagged. I'll fall asleep.

        ELEANOR
  There's a bed made up in the guest room.

ADRIAN *looks at* SAM, *and extends his arm.*

ADRIAN
Stay, Sam. I want you to stay.

SAM
All right.

SAM *sits down. They watch the TV.*

SAM (*incredulously*)
Is he crying? I think he's crying.

ELEANOR
He is.

SAM
That's extraordinary.

They continue watching. A noise from the hall of the letter-box flap opening and newspapers falling on to the floor. SAM *looks at* ELEANOR *enquiringly.*

ELEANOR (*looking at TV*)
The newspapers have arrived.

SAM
Oh. (*Beat*) Shall I get them?

ADRIAN (*looking at TV*))
No, leave them.

Nobody moves to get the newspapers. All are gazing intently at the screen. Slow fade of sound and light.

Blackout.

The End